CLOTHED FOR THE KING

The Lord wants His people to be clothed with confidence, as well as having a good and healthy countenance for Him.

ELLEN JOUBERT

© Copyright 2019 Ellen Joubert
Published by Leading Voice International Pty Ltd

All rights reserved. This book is protected by the copyright laws of Australia. This book may not be copied or reprinted for commercial gain or profit. The use of short quotations or occasional page copying for personal and group study is permitted and encouraged.

All rights reserved. Scripture quotations are taken from the online BibleGateway.com website and the different Bibles are specified in the Bibliography section.

Although every precaution has been taken to verify the accuracy of the information contained herein, the author and publisher assume no responsibility for any errors or omissions. No liability is assumed for damages that may result from the use of the information contained within.

ISBN:
Paperback
978-0-6485691-0-7

Ebook
978-0-6485691-1-4 EPUB
978-0-6485691-5-2 MOBI

I dedicate this book to Almighty God and all His people on earth. God has called me to help build His people's confidence, and I feel honoured to have been given this assignment.

As a mother, I also dedicate this book to my children, and I am praying that they will always be clothed for the King in their lives.

Love in Christ, Ellen Joubert.

TABLE OF CONTENTS

Dedication 3
Acknowledgements 7
Inspiration for the Book Title and Cover Image 9
Foreword and My Testimony. 11

CHAPTER 1
Clothed for the King 23
   An Overview of the Main Purpose and Storyline of the Bible . . .24
   Clothed with Confidence 32
   Clothed with Salvation 34
   Clothed with the Holy Spirit. 35
   Clothed with Righteousness 38
   Clothed with Health and Happiness 40
   Clothed with Prosperity 46
   Clothed with Knowledge and Wisdom 48
   Clothed with the Armour of God 52
   Clothed with Style and Beauty 56
   Clothed with Humility 58

Jesus is God who was Clothed with Humanity. 60

CHAPTER 2
There is NO Greater Love Than This! 63
    Why does the devil want to keep corrupting God's children? 64
    Do not deny your free gift in Jesus Christ from God
    the Father! 66
    Do's and Don'ts for a Prosperous Life 67

CHAPTER 3
We Belong to the King! 69
    The Feeling of Belonging 76
    Take up Your Crown 80
    God's Love Letter to You 82

CHAPTER 4
**Our Countenance and Appearance are Important
to the Lord** 85
    Jesus Christ's Magnificent Appearance
    At His Second Coming 89

CHAPTER 5
Do Everything as if You are Doing it For the Lord 93
    The Four Types of Love Described in the Bible 96
    Jesus' Second Coming 97
    My Prayer for You 102

Your Five-Week Study Guide 105
Index 129
Bibliography 136

ACKNOWLEDGEMENTS

I want to thank the following people who made it possible for me to publish *Clothed for the King*. My husband Marius Joubert, my dad Johan Moll. My friends in Christ, Nola Turner, Ruth Zanetti, and Samantha McCormack.

May the Lord bless you! May He keep you and make His face shine on you, and be gracious onto you. May He turn His face toward you and give you peace. May His plans be established and fulfilled in your life.

I love and appreciate you!

Ellen Joubert

INSPIRATION FOR THE BOOK TITLE AND COVER IMAGE

I received different feedback from people who read the book before I've published it on the book title and cover image. That is why I would like to give you the reason I had selected the title *Clothed for the King*. Some people loved it, and others did not understand it.

When the Holy Spirit prompted me to write my first Christian book, I asked God what the title should be. Then I took a quiet moment to wait on the Lord for the answer. The title *Clothed for the King* came into my mind. Because I am called to help God's children improve their appearance, this title made perfectly sense to me. It also complements my first two books that I've published which is about outer appearance, health, and building one's confidence.

When I finished writing *Clothed for the King*, confirmation came through the Holy Spirit, Scripture and sermons that to be clothed with something is a term used regularly in the Bible. Here are some scriptures:

- To be clothed with righteousness (Job 29:14, Psalm 132:9 – KJV).
- The Lord has clothed me with garments of salvation (Isaiah 61:10 – KJV).
- When Joshua was standing before the Angel of the Lord, God said to take away his filthy garments from him, and that He had removed his iniquity from him, and will clothe him with rich robes (Zechariah 3:4 – NKJV).

- David praised God for turning his mourning into dancing, taking off his sackcloth, and having clothed him with a garment of joy (Psalm 30:11 – ISV).
- When Jesus is going to return to earth, the book of Revelation describes that He will be clothed with a robe dipped in blood, and His name is called The Word of God (Revelation 19:13 – NKJV).
- All of you be submissive to one another, and be clothed with humility (1 Peter 5:5 – NKJV).
- Clothe yourself in honor and majesty (Job 40:10 – NIV).
- Meanwhile we groan, longing to be clothed instead with our heavenly dwelling, because when we are clothed, we will not be found naked (2 Corinthians 5:2-3 – NIV).
- We do not wish to be unclothed but to be clothed (2 Corinthians 5:4 – NIV).
- Instead, clothe yourselves with the Lord Jesus, and do not obey your flesh and its desires (Romans 13:14 – ISV).
- All of you who were baptised into the Messiah have clothed yourselves with the Messiah (Galatians 3:27 – ISV).
- To the disciples, Jesus said to stay in the city until they are clothed with the power from on high (Luke 24:49 – ISV).

The image on the front cover of the book has a symbolic meaning. As you will read through the book, you'll discover what it means to be clothed for the King. The king that I refer to is Jesus Christ, who will return as the King of kings. At the time of His return, He will be sitting on a white horse, clothed in a red coloured robe. Together with His armies of heaven, and His saints, He will wage war against everyone that is evil. The sword in His hand symbolises Him waging war.

We must desire to be clothed and ready for our Lord Jesus when He returns, and to be one of His saints, who will be rewarded with eternal life. The purpose of this book is to encourage you to be clothed and ready for that time. The image on the cover portrays Jesus at the time of His return, in all His glory, taking over the rulership of the earth.

FOREWORD AND MY TESTIMONY

As a believer, I know that God has ordered my steps to where I am today. After completing secondary education in South Africa, I was accepted at the *University of Pretoria (TUKS), South Africa*. I found myself amongst a group of students who were undecided about which course they wanted to study. A university representative suggested that I visit a certain college to see if I could find something there to interest me. My cousin, who was enrolled in a business course, had been telling me about a beauty technology course at the same college, and suggested I come to check it out. Thinking that this may be a sign, I went there to make inquiries and found the course had already started two weeks previously.

The college representative offered to phone the head of the department to see if she would have time to meet me, and if it would be possible that I could still enrol in the course. This was a Friday afternoon and I was able to meet with the head of the *Beauty Technology Department*. She gave me a quick run-through on what the course entailed, and it sounded like something that I would enjoy. She asked me if I could start the following Monday. I mentioned that I had to talk to my parents first, so she gave me all the relevant paperwork to take home and to complete should I decide to join the course. After a weekend of discussion with my parents, I decided to enrol in the beauty technology course. Early on the next Monday morning, I saw the head of the department again and was allowed to start that same day. The class was busy with a practical lesson when I was introduced and some ladies were puzzled as to why I started so late and thought that I must have been on holiday until then. When I said that I had seen the head of the department on Friday, and only decided over the weekend that I would enrol, they were shocked that I had been accepted on the spot. That was the first time I'd heard that there was a strict selection process to get into the course. Some had to wait two years before they were accepted. Although I did not understand it at the time, the Lord revealed to me years later that He had opened this door for me to study beauty technology.

During my third year, I also enrolled part-time in an International Modelling Academy. At the completion of the beauty technology course and the modelling course, and after three years of praying and asking the Lord to send me a good husband, He miraculously brought my husband into my life. The same cousin, who told me about the beauty technology course, in the beginning, phoned me one day. She said she entered a competition in my name to go on a three week holiday to Namibia, and I had won it. It did not sound weird to me at all because I used to enter competitions on all my family members names too. At first, I said to her that I'd rather her and her husband go on holiday. After a couple of minutes trying to convince me that only the person's name on the entry can claim the prize, she came out with the real story which goes like this.

Her husband and a friend wanted to go on a three week holiday to their home country, Namibia, and the friend did not want to be the fifth wheel on the wagon. He asked them if they knew a pleasant lady friend whom they could invite so that he at least would have someone to talk the times when they are doing their own thing. Their friend's name was Marius Joubert, and he agreed to pay for all expenses. They thought of me and that is why they made up a story so that I could not say no. Marius had never met me before, neither had I met him, but he trusted their judgment. At that stage of my life, I had never gone outside the borders of South Africa and it was an exciting offer. We would visit parts of Namibia and the Etosha National Park with all expenses paid. I accepted the offer, and before we went on the journey, Marius wanted to meet me. My cousin organised a meeting two weeks later.

The second week into our holiday Marius asked me as what would I like to see him. His question sounded a bit weird to me at first. I also didn't understand what he really meant. With some clarification, I realised he wanted to know if we were going to stay friends. After what felt like ages, out of my mouth came the word 'fiancé'. Wow! I almost dropped dead because I could not believe what I had uttered! Normally when I liked a man, I'd hide it so deep that they or anyone else could not pick up on it. He seemed okay with what I'd said, but I felt so embarrassed and did not know how to fix it. When we arrived back home from a lovely three week holiday, I told my parents that Marius had asked me to marry him. They were very surprised as it was sudden. He lived in a town which was four hours' drive from my home town and managed to visit me almost every weekend after that. During the following weeks, I had not treated Marius the best because I wanted him to pull out of the commitment to marry me. I was a very proud person then, and could not get over the fact that I actually asked him to marry me! It was better for me that he said he can't continue with our relationship than me admitting that I had made a mistake. My mother also warned me and said I must think carefully if I wanted to go ahead with the marriage because Marius was married before, and had two children. Two months after we met we got engaged, and four months after we were married. Still, the secret was kept safe that I asked him to marry me.

Soon after our wedding, I opened a modelling and deportment school, training children, from three years old through to young adults in their late twenties, for the catwalk. I helped them to build their confidence and coached them on how to improve their appearance. They performed very well in modelling and beauty competitions, but the most amazing transformation was their growth in confidence.

A year after we got married, we realised how the Lord had brought us together. Marius revealed to me that because his first wife left him for another man, he had decided never to marry again. He prayed and asked that if the Lord wanted him to ever marry again, He would make it very clear to him. After our three weeks holiday in Namibia, Marius would have gone to work as an electrician on a ship, which would have taken him away from the land for a few months at a time. He basically wanted to get away from the hurt he had gone through with a wife who had left him, and the messy divorce of trying to gain custody of his children. When I said to him I would like to see him as my fiancé, it was clear to him that this is the woman God wanted him to marry.

On my side, I met a man during my first year of studies in Pretoria, South Africa. Another cousin of mine came to visit me one day and said she was planning to move to the city. She saw an empty apartment in the block of units opposite where I lived. So we both went over to find the caretaker, to see if she could rent the apartment. The caretaker said it was already taken, but another man was moving out soon and referred us to him. My cousin could not stop talking about the handsome man we had met, and I said to her she could go for him as I am not interested. At the time I was an introvert and she was an extrovert. I knew then to never try and compete with her for a man as it could turn out disastrous. They kept in contact after that first meeting, and he also asked her where I lived. So we became friends. For the following three years we had an on and off friendship because we both were busy studying. In the end, I did fall head over heels for him. During that time he was also in an on and off relationship with his ex-girlfriend. I never really had any serious relationships before and had no experience to fight for a man. At the end of my third year, I went on my knees and asked God that if this man is not for me, that He send me the man He wanted me to marry. I asked for a godly man who loved God and would grow with me in His ways. That is what God did for me! He made my cousin arrange a meeting with Marius Joubert and the holiday that followed.

As I grew spiritually during the first year of married life, I realised that the Holy Spirit must have talked through my mouth saying to Marius that I would like to see him as my fiancé. Marius knew all along that God had made it very clear for him to marry me. He was spiritually much more mature than I was at that time. From that point onwards, I realised how God worked miraculously to bring us two together, and I wanted to know more about God. I was not shy anymore to tell others that I actually asked Marius to marry me and how it happened. My parents were the first people to know the truth.

A few years later, while I was still running my modelling and deportment school, my life took a dramatic turn when I committed my life to the Lord and only wanted to learn about and serve Almighty God. I was pregnant with our first child and a few months after our daughter's birth in 1994, I handed the modelling and deportment school over to someone else. My husband had also been offered another job, that came with a comfortable house, which was part of a close-knit community of thirteen houses, offices, and warehouses in the grounds of a power station. There were no shops or cafes in this village, and the closest small country town was about seven kilometres away with only limited supplies available. This gave me enough quiet time to bring up our daughter and study the Word of God. Just before our daughter, Ellen Jr. turned two, I gave birth to our second daughter, Maria, in 1996.

During 1998, my husband Marius had a dream from the Lord that we should move to Australia. Although very keen at the time, I got cold feet and talked him out of it. One day in 1999 while I was studying my Bible, I heard the Holy Spirit say that I would write books in the future. I was amazed, because I did briefly think about it after completing my studies, but had moved it to the back of my mind as life continued. We lived in this close-knit community for years before my husband was transferred to a bigger town as a supervisor, where he managed a depot for South Africa's national power provider. It was a privilege to have been a stay-at-home mum for the first years of our daughters' lives.

When we arrived in this new town at the beginning of 2001, I was offered a job as an advertising consultant for the local newspaper. For the following five years the Lord taught me and made me stronger for the life ahead. During 2005 I was ready to move and asked my husband to arrange our immigration to Australia. On the 16th of June 2006, we landed in Sydney. This new life was not without its challenges, and within three months we travelled 3934 kilometres by car to Perth in Western Australia, where we have been ever since. From 2008 to 2016 I worked as an advertising representative in the newspaper industry. I loved my job and learned so much during these eight years during which I experienced the most personal growth of my lifetime. I enjoyed it so much that I made up my mind to work there until I retired. However, around 2013 the company went through a huge loss in market share and had to restructure. Unfortunately for the employees, the company did not follow fair practices and used unconventional ways to minimize the workforce. It was during 2013 that I once again recommitted my life to the Lord, and realised that I did not want to work in that environment. I told my husband that I wanted to return to the Spiritual level I was at when we left South Africa, and continue on from there. I hoped that he would join me. To start life over in a new country takes a lot of time and effort and it is easy not to stay connected with God. My husband agreed, so we called our daughters, who were in their late teens, and explained to them what we had decided, inviting them to join us. They agreed, and all four of us pursued God from that point onwards. It was during this time that I asked God to open another door for me so that I could be around like-minded people. I only wanted to live to serve Him and did not want to be caught up in all the unfairness and struggles of working in an environment where God is not acknowledged. It hurt me when people mocked God, and I felt powerless knowing that there was nothing I could do about it. Only God can change the hearts of people with that attitude.

While I worked as an advertising representative, there were times when God felt far away. A few times I asked Him why? I felt lost, like a ship without a rudder. I had no idea where I was going! He spoke to my heart that there is a time for everything and that I was going through a training season. He said that the time would come when He would feel very close again. I realised afterwards that if I had been in that intimate space with the Lord as when we left South Africa, I would not have lasted long as an advertising representative. On the other hand, I would not have something to build from if I had not worked for those eight years in the newspaper industry. Having recommitted my life to the Lord, I only wanted to live for Him and did not want to be part of this carnal world. I have listened to many testimonies of people who went to heaven, either in a dream, or when they died and were sent back to life to testify about heaven and God's Glory. They all said that they did not want to come back to earth. That is why I believe God sometimes has to minimise that strong spiritual connection with Him, otherwise, we would not want to work and fulfil our assignment for Him here on earth. I'm not saying that we must not pursue a strong relationship with the Lord, because He wants us to be close to Him. I believe there are levels of spiritual connection with Jesus for certain times in our life, and for certain assignments that He gives us. When you feel there is a disconnection in your spiritual life with the Lord, despite all your efforts to stay close to Him, hang in there, because you may be in a training season.

Many times the Lord wants us to be trained in worldly things in order to be equipped for His purposes. We will only leave this world when we pass on to heaven. Being in the world, and concerned with worldly things such as working to earn a living, going to the doctor if we are feeling sick and have not been healed through prayer. These are things that we cannot escape from while we are on earth. We must decide how we want to prioritise our lives. Are we only going to chase fame and fortune, or are we going to listen to God's instilled voice to have the right balance in our lives?

During 2015 while I was still working as an advertising representative, I asked the Lord why it was that when He had opened doors for me to become a beauty therapist, hairdresser, and modelling trainer, I found myself doing something totally different. I told Him that it felt like such a waste of the years that I had spent studying for these qualifications when I was convinced at the time that He had opened for me. I was not working in any of these professions, and I really missed training kids and young adults to help build their confidence. I wondered where I would have been if I kept the modelling and deportment school. I thought maybe I had been mistaken all those years ago in thinking that God opened the doors for me.

On the 18th of March 2016, I was worked out of my position as a Senior Advertising Executive in an unconventional way. It was unexpected and painful to see people I had trusted, act with an ulterior motive. I knew God was in control. If it was not for my awesome family who supported me through it all, it would have been devastating. We could all feel God's assurance and guidance through this uncertain time. On the other hand, it was I who asked God to open another door for me in the first place. The wonderful thing about it all was that God gave me the ability to step out as a winner from this company. Praise God for His favour! I knew that if we asked God to open another door for us, we needed to accept the fact that it may not be all smooth sailing. He will always give us the strength and peace to close a door before He opens a new one. The Word of God promises us in Proverbs 3:5-6 that if we trust in the Lord with all our heart, and not lean on our own understanding, and that we will acknowledge Him in all our ways, that He will direct our paths. I would like to encourage the reader to also find peace and rest for your life in God, trusting Him in the good times and the bad.

While I was going through this horrible work experience at the end of my time in the newspaper industry, I received a prophetic word which said "Do not forget about your dreams!" I knew God was speaking to my heart, as I felt and heard my heart pumping in my chest. I had to think for a moment what my dreams were because I had so many. I asked the Lord which dreams He wanted me to pursue, and He spoke to my heart saying "I want you to help build My people's confidence". It is God who puts dreams in our hearts and minds. The enemy lies to many of God's children, telling them they are ugly and unworthy, which affects their confidence.

I suddenly became aware of how God had ordered my steps when I qualified as a beauty therapist, hairdresser, and modelling trainer. It all made sense, and I realised I was in training all those years to get ready for the assignment He had planned for me all along. It was to help people build their confidence by teaching them how to improve their countenance and appearance. Some may think that these are all worldly things which do not really matter, but the Lord showed me that He loves us all so much, and has made us all beautiful and worthy. The enemy of God and His children try very hard to make people lose confidence and feel unworthy. A lack of knowledge of how to improve one's appearance, and a busy life, are contributing factors to why some people lost their desire to invest time in their appearance. Some even went as far as to give up in life. Others lost their confidence because of how they had been treated in life, and do not know how to get it back.

While I was running a twelve-week confidence-building course for teenage girls, during the first half of 2017, I decided to write a book that would complement my workshops. This book is called *Style Yourself with Confidence*. It is a practical guide for women, with two hundred and fifty-five illustrations and colour images, teaching how to best style their body shape and features. Learning these styling techniques help build confidence. The enemy keeps attacking our minds by making us believe we are not good enough. We compare ourselves with others, and to the image that the media portrays of the perfect man or woman. As soon as we start loving ourselves as we are, our mind changes from a negative to a more positive view.

When we feel negative and defeated, we do not even feel like getting out of bed in the morning, but when we are positive, no matter what is happening, it feels like we can take on any obstacle!

At the end of my book *Style Yourself with Confidence,* I talk about how to handle bullying. Although this is not a Christian book, I could feel God's help in preparing it for publishing. It was written for all the women in this world, no matter what their age or nationality. God loves every person equally, even though some do not want to acknowledge Him. That is why I have written *Style Yourself with Confidence* for the general market because God loves all. When the book was almost ready for publishing, the Holy Spirit brought to my remembrance the prophecy He gave me in 1999, that I would write books one day. I was humbled to realise that God had entrusted me to build His children's confidence through my books and seminars.

At the beginning of March 2018, while this first book was still in production, the Holy Spirit prompted me to start writing the second book. I felt He was urging me to complete it quickly, and I finished *How to Look and Feel Younger for Longer* in two and a half months. This book includes sixty-eight images, which took some time to edit for a quality production. It was written to help people know that with everyday practices they can look and feel younger for longer, no matter what age or gender they are. It shows how to improve your countenance and appearance, and also how to keep the body healthy through correct diet and exercise. After it was published in October 2018, God inspired me to write *Clothed for the King,* to explain why our countenance and appearance are important to Him.

To my readers, I just want to say that I feel honoured. I really hope my books will mean something to you and will help you build confidence, in yourself and in life. For young readers, I pray that you will be inspired to make informed decisions in your life so that you never get to a point where you feel ugly, unworthy and unloved. God loves you so much, and just as He has given us His Word (The

Bible) to guide us through life, He also encourages people in different walks of life, to share their knowledge to uplift His people.

Thank you for reading my testimony! To those of you who are still searching to find your place in this world, my prayer is that through life's journey you will find God. That you will recognize the doors that He has already opened for you, and will continue to open, to guide you on the right path that He has planned for you.

Love in Christ
Ellen Joubert

CHAPTER 1

Clothed for the King

When we are to meet a king or the President of a country, we make sure we look good for the occasion. We may even get a new haircut, take our outfit to the dry cleaners, get our make-up done, book in for a manicure and pedicure, and maybe even buy new shoes. Because kings and presidents have great power, it is a huge privilege to meet them. We'll be on our best behaviour and make sure that we look our best.

How would you feel to meet the King of all kings one day? The Bible describes Jesus Christ our Lord and Saviour as the King of kings, and the Lord of lords. Revelation 17:14 states "They will wage war against the Lamb, but the Lamb will triumph over them because he is Lord of lords and King of kings, and with Him will be his called, chosen and faithful followers". The Lamb referred to here is Jesus. Revelation 19:16 says "On his robe and on his thigh, he has this name written: KING OF KINGS AND LORD OF LORDS. So how much more should we want to look our best when we meet the King of kings, who is Jesus Christ our Lord and Creator!

When I meet people who do not believe in Jesus Christ and what He has accomplished for us, I realised that the reason they do not believe is that they never had the opportunity to read or learn about what Christianity and the Bible are all about. We cannot judge a person if they have never heard the story of salvation and Jesus. On the other hand, how can people pass judgment on Christianity if they have not done a proper investigation of it? If someone tells me that my decision on something can determine if I would live forever or not, I would investigate it further to come to the truth. When a child grows up, he or she is usually the product of their parents and circumstances. Many times what we have been taught or gone through during our growing years, determine who we are and what we become. When we have been taught there is no God, it is very hard to believe otherwise. Those who grew up in a Christian home are very blessed because they started life on the right foundation. What a shame though when they then turn away from that foundation and say, 'I do not believe there is a God who created all things'.

I always try to give a short explanation to a person who does not know anything about the Bible, about how Jesus Christ, the Son of God, came to earth to restore our relationship with God. It has taken me my whole life to know what the Bible is about, and to understand that it contains the true words and guidance of God. It can only take a short explanation to help someone else understand the basics of the Bible, so that it will be easier for them to read it afterwards. Where possible, I give them a Bible, so that they can go through it in their own time. For those of you who do not know the story of Jesus Christ, I will explain it briefly in the next passage.

An Overview of the Main Purpose and Storyline of the Bible

In the beginning, God created the heavens and the earth. The earth and everything in it were created in six days. The second verse of Genesis Chapter 1, describes the earth as formless and empty. Darkness was over the surface of the deep, and the Spirit of God hovered over the waters. On Day One, God said "Let there be light", and He separated the light from the darkness. God called the light 'day' and the darkness 'night'. On Day Two He said "Let there be a vault between the waters to separate water from water". God called the vault 'sky'. On Day Three God said, "Let the water under the sky be gathered to one place, and let dry ground appear". God called the dry ground 'land' and the gathered waters under the sky 'seas'. He also said, "Let the land produce vegetation: plants and trees on the land that bear fruit with seed in it, according to their various kinds." And it was so. On Day Four, God said, "Let there be lights in the vault of the sky to separate the day from the night, and let them serve as signs to mark seasons, and days and years, and let them be lights in the vault of the sky to give light on the earth." On Day Five, God created all the sea creatures and birds. God blessed them and said, "Be fruitful and increase in number and fill the water in the seas, and let the birds increase on the earth." On Day Six, God created all the animals on the land. From livestock to wild animals and creatures on the ground, each was created according to its kind. Still on Day Six, God said in Genesis 1:26, "Let us make mankind in our image, in our likeness, so that they may rule over the fish in the sea and the birds in the sky, over the livestock and all the wild animals, and over all the creatures that move along the ground." God blessed them and said to them, "Be fruitful and increase in number; fill the earth and subdue it". God is Love and he wanted a family. That is why He created mankind in His own image. Genesis 1:27 says "So God created mankind in His own image, in the image of God He created them; male and female He created them." When God finished creating the earth and everything in it, verse 31 says "God saw everything that He had made, and behold, it was very good."

When we come to Genesis 2:1-3 we read "Thus the heavens and the earth were completed in all their vast array. By the seventh day, God had finished the work He had been doing; so on the seventh day, He rested from all his work. Then God blessed the seventh day and made it holy because on it He rested from all the work of creating that he had done." In Genesis 2 the author gives a more detailed description of the creation of plants, trees, the man, and the animals. Genesis 2:5-7 says "Now no shrub had yet appeared on the earth and no plant had yet sprung up, for the Lord God had not sent rain on the earth and there was no one to work the ground, but streams came up from the earth and watered the whole surface of the ground. Then the Lord God formed a man from the dust of the ground and breathed into his nostrils the breath of life, and the man became a living being."

In the beginning, mankind was created in God's image, and was still in a spiritual form (spirit) because in verse five it says '...and there was no one to work the ground.' In verse seven of the King James Version, it says that the Lord God formed man of the dust of the ground (body), and breathed into his nostrils the breath of life, and man became a living soul (soul). Therefore mankind was created in three stages: spirit, body, and soul. God then planted a garden in the east called Eden, where He put the man He had formed to work it and take care of it. God then told the man in Genesis 2:16-17, "You are free to eat from any tree in the garden; but you must not eat from the tree of the knowledge of good and evil, for when you eat from it you will certainly die."

Genesis 2:18 describes that when God made the man, He realised it was not good for him to be alone and He said He would make him a suitable helper. In Genesis 2:19-20 God formed every beast of the field, and every fowl of the air out of the ground and brought them to Adam so that he could name them. Whatever name Adam called each living creature was its name. God named the man Adam before He brought all the animals to him to be named. God gave Adam dominion over all the animals. In verse 20 we read "...But for Adam, no suitable helper was found." At this stage, God created Eve as a suitable helper.

Genesis 2:21-22 says "So the Lord God caused the man to fall into a deep sleep; and while he was sleeping, he took one of his ribs and then closed up the place with flesh. Then the Lord God made a woman from the rib he had taken out of the man, and he brought her to the man." Adam and his wife were both naked but felt no shame.

Genesis 3 describes the 'fall of mankind' and why it became necessary for the Son of God (Jesus Christ), to come to earth as a man to be crucified for the sin that had become part of mankind's nature. Verse one says that the serpent was more crafty than any of the wild animals the Lord God had made, and he said to the woman "Did God really say, you must not eat from any tree in the garden?" Here we realise that the devil was talking through the serpent to confuse the woman.

Genesis 3:2-23 explains how our relationship with God was compromised "The woman said to the serpent, We may eat fruit from the trees in the garden, but God did say, 'You must not eat fruit from the tree that is in the middle of the garden, and you must not touch it, or you will die.' 'You will not certainly die,' the serpent said to the woman. 'For God knows that when you eat from it your eyes will be opened, and you will be like God, knowing good and evil.' When the woman saw that the fruit of the tree was good for food and pleasing to the eye, and also desirable for gaining wisdom, she took some and ate it. She also gave some to her husband, who was with her, and he ate it. Then the eyes of both of them were opened, and they realised they were naked; so they sewed fig leaves together and made coverings for themselves. Then the man and his wife heard the sound of the Lord God as He was walking in the garden in the cool of the day, and they hid from the Lord God among the trees of the garden. But the Lord God called to the man, 'Where are you?' He answered, 'I heard you in the garden, and I was afraid because I was naked; so I hid.' And God said, 'Who told you that you were naked? Have you eaten from the tree that I commanded you not to eat from?' The man said, 'The woman you put here with me – she gave me some fruit from the tree, and I ate it.' Then the Lord God said to the woman, 'What is this you have done?' The woman said, 'The serpent deceived me, and I ate.' So the Lord God said to the serpent, 'Because you have done this, cursed are you above all livestock and all wild animals! You will crawl on your belly and you will eat dust all the days of your life. And I will put enmity between you and the woman, and between your offspring and hers; he will crush your head, and you will strike his heel.' To the woman he said, 'I will make your pains in childbearing very severe; with painful labour you will give birth to children. Your desire will be for your husband, and he will rule over you.' To Adam he said, 'Because you listened to your wife and ate fruit from the tree about which I commanded you, you must not eat from, cursed is the ground because of you; through painful toil you will eat food from it all the days of your life. It will produce thorns and thistles for you, and you will eat the plants of the field. By the sweat of your brow you will eat your food until you return to the ground, since from it you were taken; for dust you are and to dust you will return.' Adam named his wife Eve, because she would become the mother of all the living. The Lord God made garments of skin for Adam and his wife and clothed them. And the Lord God said, 'The man has now become like one of us, knowing good and evil. He must not be allowed to reach out his hand and take also from the tree of life and eat, and live forever.' So the Lord God banished him from the Garden of Eden to work the ground from which he had been taken."

The 'fall of mankind' means that not only Adam and Eve fell, but all future generations born from them also fell. So that every child from thereon was born in the fallen state. After this, Adam and Eve were removed from the Garden of Eden, where they had been in regular fellowship with God. Their face-to-face relationship with God could not continue. Isaiah 59:2 says that our iniquities have separated us from God, and because of our sins He has hidden His face from us.

I asked God a few times why He does not stop all the evil and madness of this world? The answer is: He did! He gave us the Bible which is the blueprint of how to live a happy and successful life and stay away from everything that is evil. Many people are ignorant and would rather enjoy what this world offers, than to spend time knowing the blueprint that God has given His people.

It is believed that Adam was around a hundred and thirty years old when he ate the fruit given to him by Eve, from the tree of the knowledge of good and evil. From this point to the birth of Jesus; God, Jesus and the Holy Spirit only appeared to those to whom they chose to appear. All of mankind on the earth was in this fallen state until Jesus Christ was crucified which reversed the curse. While Jesus lived among the people during His earthly life, God and the Holy Spirit continued to visit the prophets and anointed people, as well as Jesus Christ. The people on the earth before Jesus could only hear from God through the priests, prophets and His anointed people. The only way to make atonement for their sins during that time was by sacrificing unblemished animals, so that when God accepted their offering, their sins were forgiven. Thank God He had the perfect plan to wash away mankind's sin forever, otherwise, the family He created would have all perished. That is why He sent His only begotten Son to earth to die for our sins through a humiliating, harsh and painful death on the cross. Jesus died once for all, to restore our relationship with God the Father. The death and resurrection of Jesus gave us the opportunity to live with Him in heaven for eternity. Jesus lived on earth for around thirty-three years before He was crucified. People could also hear from God directly through Jesus Christ's teachings, during His life on earth.

In the first four books of the New Testament, we read all about Jesus Christ's life. These 'gospel books' are attributed to the disciples Matthew, Mark, Luke, and John. Each of the books tells the story of Jesus in a different way. Each disciple tells us how they experienced moving around with Jesus. They were witnesses of what they heard and what they saw while Jesus was with them.

Three days after Jesus was crucified, He was raised from the dead by the Holy Spirit. During these three days since He was crucified, until He was raised, He first went to heaven to God the Father, giving himself as atonement for all sin that was, is, and is to come. He also went to Hades or the Sheol which is a place of the dead, a darkness where all the dead people go who were disobedient. Hades is a place of stillness and darkness cut off from life, and separated from God. Jesus went to Hades to take over the kingdom of Satan. He was also preaching to the 'spirits in prison' during these three days according to 1 Peter 3:18-19. In Matthew 12:40 we read the following "For as Jonas was three days and three nights in the whale's belly; so shall the Son of man be three days and three nights in the heart of the earth". Jesus' victory on the cross has given Him the authority over death and the place of the dead (Hades). He alone can determine who will enter death and Hades, and who will come out.

After these three days Jesus came back to earth for a period of forty days as the Bible describes it, where He appeared to hundreds of other people who also witnessed that He was raised from the dead. After forty days on earth, he was taken up into heaven where he sits at the right hand of God. When He ascended to heaven, He promised to give us the gift of the Holy Spirit, to live inside us when we accept Him. The Holy Spirit is our direct link to God the Father and Jesus Christ. It is wonderful that God loves His children so much, that He went to such lengths to correct what the devil had corrupted.

When God's children begin to understand the Bible's amazing stories and teachings, life starts to make more sense. God's indwelling Spirit inspired people to write down what they witnessed for future generations. It is a fascinating subject. If you really want to know more about the Bible to be encouraged, I urge you to research it for yourself, with the help of the Holy Spirit. Only He can give revelation. You will be amazed at how events, dates, and prophecies fit perfectly like a puzzle.

Ten key components of how to be clothed for our King

- *Clothed with Confidence.*
  Firstly our Spiritual identity comes from God, how He created us. We need to have that confidence in who we are created to be.

- *Clothed with Salvation.*
  God, out of mercy and grace, has clothed us in Christ which is the garment of salvation.

- *Clothed with the Holy Spirit.*
  When a person gives his or her life to Jesus Christ, they receive the Holy Spirit as a gift who will connect them to God the Father and Jesus.

- *Clothed with righteousness.*
  Being righteous means to live right, especially in a moral way. A righteous person not only does the right thing for other people but also follows the laws, and ways of God, as explained in the Bible.

- *Clothed with health and happiness.*
  A healthy body and mind will help build our confidence. This will require some work on our part to create a healthy body through a healthy diet, regular exercise, and developing our intellect.

- *Clothed with prosperity.*
  Prosperity includes financial stability, happiness and health. To prosper in life we have to give God the reigns over our life and finances.

- *Clothed with knowledge and wisdom.*
  Through gaining the right knowledge in life, we'll be able to stand strong in this imperfect world. Worldly wisdom comes

from knowledge. Spiritual wisdom comes from the Holy Spirit and the Word of God.

- *Clothed with the Armour of God.*
  In short, the Armour of God comes through learning the truths that God gave us in the Bible. These truths will give us the right knowledge on how to protect ourselves against harm from our enemies, including the devil and his demons.

- *Clothed with style and beauty.*
  Our body is the temple of God's indwelling Holy Spirit today. Therefore God wants us to be beautiful and well cared for. We must represent Him well on this earth.

- *Clothed with humility.*
  Humility means to be meek and humble. Submitting yourself to God and others. Admitting to God you are a sinner and you need His forgiveness. Nor comparing yourself to others. Spending more time listening and encouraging others, than talking about, or praising yourself.

Clothed with Confidence

As you have read through the previous passage explaining how Almighty God (God the Father, God the Son, and God the Holy Spirit) created the earth, we see in Genesis 1:26 that God said 'let us' make mankind in 'our image', in 'our likeness'. This shows clearly that the Trinity worked together when everything on earth was created. What a privilege to be created in the image and likeness of the Trinity! This doesn't mean that God is a physical being with two arms, two legs, and a human head. Although we know Jesus as a human being during His 'First Coming', and for the sake of explaining the image and likeness of God, we know it has a much deeper meaning than physical appearance. It is saying that we have characteristics of God.

For example, we have similar intellect, a will, and emotions. In the Bible, God is sometimes portrayed as sad, hurt, angry or joyful. These are the same emotions that we experience.

Because God gave us a free will, we make decisions on a daily basis, just as God makes decisions regularly as described throughout the Bible. We have a natural creative ability and appreciation for the arts like music, dance, literature, painting, drawing, or sculpting, just like God when He created the heavens and the earth. When you look at all the different nationalities in the world, you'll notice that every nation has certain physical characteristics identifying them as part of a specific nation.

Acts 17:26 describes it beautifully how we all came from one man, Adam, "From one man He made all the nations, that they should inhabit the whole earth; and he marked out their appointed times in history and the boundaries of their lands." This demonstrates God's amazing creativity and artistry. No one knows what nationality Adam and Eve were, but we do know from this scripture that all nationalities came from them. Racism, therefore, is invented by Satan to divide God's children and breaking down their confidence! As children of God we must not judge people according to their nationality, but by their works and character. God is continuously creating. Revelation 21 tells us that at the end of the world God will create a new heaven and a new earth. The Bible also tells us that God is LOVE and that He created us to have a relationship with Him. This is why we always need love and a sense of belonging. We cannot live happily without good relationships with our spouse, children, family, and friends. All people desire approval and love from birth.

We are so much more than we realise. Our identity comes from God Almighty. Satan knows that we have great potential, and has been working since the beginning of time to destroy mankind's identity and confidence in Almighty God. When a person loses confidence, their whole identity is affected. Think of when someone loses the memory of who they are, how confused and unhappy they are. They have no idea where to go from there. The only option is to regain the memory of who they are or to start a new memory. Only then will they be able to move forward. Almighty God our Creator loves us so much and He wants us to be clothed with confidence, knowing who we are and where we came from.

In worldly terms, when we are confident, we feel satisfied and happy with who we are. In spiritual terms, the Holy Spirit gives us our identity and confidence in God.

With confidence, we will overcome negative thoughts and obstacles. Even if we are not perfect by worldly standards, we will be content with who we are and who God created us to be. The world we live in is very carnal, meaning that feelings and desires are more physical than spiritual. Many people feel confident when they know they are beautiful or handsome, live in a beautiful house and/or suburb, drive a sports car, have plenty of money, go on regular overseas holidays. When they realise that these carnal feelings and material possessions do not determine who they are, and that they are created in God's own image, all these worldly things become less important. An intimate relationship with Jesus is worth more than all these things. By accepting Jesus into our heart and life, we receive the Holy Spirit to live inside us, connecting us to Jesus and God the Father. Our confidence then comes from the Holy Spirit, giving us our identity in Christ Jesus.

Clothed with Salvation

Out of mercy and grace, God has clothed us with Christ which is the 'garment of salvation'. Salvation is the clothing appropriate for coming into God's presence. Such clothing is not something that we ourselves can make or purchase, but it is prepared and provided by God through Jesus Christ.

In the beginning, Adam and Eve tried to clothe themselves in fig leaves, after they have sinned, and that could not make them feel whole again. God had to slay two innocent animals, and made coats of the skins to clothe them.

One day, when the marriage of the Lamb (Jesus) will come, His bride (The Church) must be clothed in fine linen, clean and white. Fine linen stands for the righteous acts of God's holy people (Revelation 19:7-8).

In the New Testament 'salvation' mostly refers to eternal deliverance from hell. In the Old Testament, it was more likely to be referring to a temporal deliverance from danger. When David was on the run from his enemies, he would pray, 'Save me, God', meaning simply, 'Keep me safe from the people who are trying to kill me'.

Clothed with the Holy Spirit

After Jesus was crucified and raised from the dead, He ascended to heaven to sit at the right hand of God the Father. When He left, He promised to send us the Comforter (Holy Spirit). In John 16:7 Jesus said: "Nevertheless I tell you the truth; It is expedient for you that I go away: for if I go not away, the Comforter will not come unto you; but if I depart, I will send him unto you". With the help of the Holy Spirit, we begin to recognize that there is so much more to life than riches and fame. Of all the gifts and blessings that God gives His people, there is none greater than the gift of the Holy Spirit. The functions of the Holy Spirit are described in John 16:8-15 when Jesus said to His disciples "When He comes, He will prove the world to be in the wrong about sin and righteousness and judgment: about sin, because people do not believe in Me; about righteousness, because I am going to the Father, where you can see Me no longer; and about judgment, because the prince of this world now stands condemned. I have much more to say to you, more than you can now bear. But when He, the Spirit of truth, comes, He will guide you into all the truth. He will not speak on his own; He will speak only what He hears, and He will tell you what is yet to come. He will glorify Me because it is from Me that He will receive what He will make known to you. All that belongs to the Father is Mine. That is why I said the Spirit will receive from Me what He will make known to you."

The Holy Spirit will also give us that assurance in our heart that we are saved. Through the Holy Spirit's confirmation, we 'know that we know' that if we die today, we will go to heaven. This is a confidence that the devil cannot take away from us. Usually, this spiritual confidence also brings acceptance of ourselves the way God has created us, and we do not desire to be like the world's standards. Romans 8:16 says "The Spirit himself testifies with our spirit that we are God's children". If you have accepted Jesus Christ as your Lord and Saviour, but do not have this full assurance in your heart, study The Word of God every day, because by hearing the words of God, you'll come to know the truth of God's promises. John 8:31-32 give us this revelation when Jesus said, "If you abide in My Word, you are truly My disciples, and you will know the truth, and the truth will set you free."

If you have not yet accepted Jesus Christ as your Lord and Saviour, read the following prayers out loud and mean it from your heart. It must be read out loud so that the devil and all spiritual forces of evil in the world and heavenly realms can hear that you have become a true child of Almighty God. Even our Lord Jesus would love to hear that you are not shy to proclaim Him as your Lord and Saviour. In Matthew 10:33 Jesus says "But whoever disowns me before others, I will disown before my Father in heaven."

Romans 10:9 also says that if you declare with your mouth, "Jesus is Lord," and believe in your heart that God raised Him from the dead, you will be saved.

The Sinners Prayer

Dear Lord Jesus, I am a sinner who has broken your laws which have separated me from You. Please forgive all my sins and help me to avoid sinning again. Protect me from all evil as my life continues from this point on. I believe that you, Jesus Christ, are the only begotten Son of God the Father, who came to earth to be crucified for my sins. You were raised from the dead by the power of the Holy Spirit and are now sitting at the right hand of Almighty God in heaven. Lord Jesus, I invite You into my heart to guide me in your perfect ways. Make known to me the future and show me the path You have ordained for me. I love you Lord and thank you for your huge sacrifice to restore my relationship with God our Father.

I pray this in Jesus wonderful Name.
Amen and Amen!

A Prayer for Salvation

Have mercy on me, O God, according to Your unfailing love; according to Your great compassion blot out my transgressions. Wash away all my iniquity and cleanse me from my sin. For I know my transgressions, and my sin is always before me. Against You, You only, have I sinned and done what is evil in Your sight; so You are right in Your verdict and justified when You judge. Surely I was sinful at birth, sinful from the time my mother conceived me. Yet you desired faithfulness even in the womb; You taught me wisdom in that secret place. Cleanse me with hyssop, and I will be clean; wash me, and I will be whiter than snow. Let me hear joy and gladness; let the bones you have crushed rejoice. Hide Your face from my sins and blot out all my iniquity. Create in me a pure heart, O God, and renew a steadfast spirit within me. Do not cast me from Your presence or take Your Holy Spirit from me. Restore to me the joy of Your salvation and grant me a willing spirit, to sustain me. Then I will teach transgressors Your ways, so that sinners will turn back to You. Deliver me from the guilt of bloodshed, O God, You who are God my Saviour and my tongue will sing of Your righteousness. Open my lips, Lord, and my mouth will declare Your praise. You do not delight in sacrifice, or I would bring it; You do not take pleasure in burnt offerings. My sacrifice, O God, is a broken spirit; a broken and contrite heart You, God, will not despise - Psalm 51:1-17 NIV.

Amen and Amen!

Clothed with Righteousness

A person who knows the Lord should have works of righteousness. Righteousness is closely related to our character. In other words, it is who we are, what we think, and what we do. In Matthew 7:15-20 we read how we'll know people by their fruits (their characteristics and actions), especially those who proclaim to be teachers in the Word of God. "Beware of false prophets, who come to you in sheep's clothing, but inwardly they are ravenous wolves. You will know them by their fruits. Do men gather grapes from thornbushes or figs from thistles? Even so, every good tree bears good fruit, but a bad tree bears bad fruit. A good tree cannot bear bad fruit, nor can a bad tree bear good fruit. Every tree that does not bear good fruit is cut down and thrown into the fire. Therefore by their fruits you will know them."

That is why it is important that you study the Word of God yourself as well and not just take your preacher's word for it. One of Satan's plans is to keep the words of God out of your heart. We should study the Bible and memorize as many scriptures as we can, so that it can come forth in times of difficulty, when we can proclaim the scriptures out loud to break the power of the devil and his demons that are coming against us. The Bible is written symbolically and in parables with a lot of cross-referencing. When you study to understand it, and are not just reading it to get the job done, then God can open it up for you. Of course, we sometimes need to listen to speakers, and read books written by other godly people to break open the scriptures, so that we can understand it better. However we have to be careful whose teachings we listen to, because some may not teach you the truths of the Bible correctly. As soon as you start to understand it better, get on with your own Bible study and always ask the Holy Spirit, who is within you, to teach you God's Word so that you'll grow in godly wisdom.

God teaches us to be righteous and to bear good fruits. Galatians 5:22-24 declares that the fruit of the Spirit is love, joy, peace, forbearance, kindness, goodness, faithfulness, gentleness and self-control. Those who belong to Christ Jesus have crucified the flesh with its passions and desires.

According to Galatians 5:19-21 the acts of the flesh, also known as bad fruits, are sexual immorality, impurity, debauchery, idolatry, witchcraft, hatred, discord, jealousy, fits of rage, selfish ambition, dissensions, factions, envy, drunkenness, orgies, and the like. Jesus warns us that those who live like this will not inherit the kingdom of God.

Psalm 37:37 says: "Mark the perfect man, and behold the upright, for the end of that man is peace." This is the inheritance or birthright of righteous men and women. They enjoy peace in their life. There is no peace for those who break God's laws, or the believers who pretend to worship God. God is looking for men and women who feel the heartbeat of Him to bring peace to the world. His heart beats for souls and is looking for men and women with integrity and honesty, not pretenders.

Some Churches are weak because their ministers and believers are dabbling in the occult and secret societies, or they are involved in sexual misconduct, or are pursuing money instead of souls. Some believers are lying and living in sin. Sunday after Sunday they will go to Church, but they remain the same. They are believers who have no commitment to Bible study, prayer meetings or evangelism; all which are the heartbeat of God. This is why some Churches are so powerless to heal or save today. As long as believers are living sinful lifestyles in secret or openly, they will never have the power of the anointing or the fullness of the Holy Spirit.

Clothed with Health and Happiness

It is important to God that we know how to look after our earthly body or temple of the Holy Spirit. Our confidence can be affected by: How we look, our health, our happiness, our financial status, our intellect, our spiritual growth and our sense of security. The devil is real, and because he hates God and all His children, he tries everything in his power to hurt us. In John 10:10 Jesus says "The thief comes only to steal and kill and destroy; I have come that they may have life, and have it to the full". The word 'thief' refers to the devil. He attacks us, so that we lose confidence in God and in life. The insecurity of being unsure about how we look and the feeling that we are not good enough, are thoughts that the devil usually tricks us with. It can come as hurtful words of others, or through the devil whispering in our ear, and through the abuse of others. Many health issues come from the devil, but some health issues arise from wrong eating habits, not enough exercise, addictions, and too much unhealthy stress in our lives.

Our confidence originates from our mind, that is our brain. Most of the time when the Bible refers to our heart, it is actually referring to our mind, which is influenced by our six senses; sight (eyes), hearing (ears), smell (nose), taste (tongue), touch and feeling (skin), and our sixth sense (the Holy Spirit living inside of us). There are other senses inside the body like hunger, thirst, vibration, balance etc; but these six major senses contribute to help build our confidence. What you watch, read, and listen to, will affect your mood and shape your character. Our brain is a very complex organ which is designed to control all our bodily functions. It can be seen as our body's computer making sure everything runs effectively and efficiently, even when we are asleep. The brain is so powerful that it can even heal the body from illnesses. That is how wonderfully God has created us. If you study the brain and its functions, you'll realise that it must have been created by an Almighty God, and couldn't just come into existence on its own. When someone is brain-dead, it means that the brain is injured and no longer works. The other organs in the body are also vital for living, but when the brain is affected it will create a chain of negative reactions in the body. The first five senses work in sync with the brain. Stimuli through the senses are sent to the brain, processed, and sent back to the particular body part so that we can make sense of the world around us.

A healthy brain will produce a healthy and happy life. In order to maintain good general health we have to drink enough water every day; get enough oxygen through good breathing techniques and exercise; reading, listening, and watching positive materials that will promote intellectual growth and healthy thoughts; and a life without constant stress and worries. When you enter God's perfect peace and rest, it will create a healthy body and brain, eliminating anxiety and mental illnesses. Jesus says to us in John 16:33 "These things I have spoken to you, that in Me you may have peace. In the world you will have tribulation; but be of good cheer, I have overcome the world." In Philippians 4:6-7 we read "Be anxious for nothing, but in everything by prayer and supplication, with thanksgiving, let your requests be made known to God; and the peace of God, which surpasses all understanding, will guard your hearts and minds through Christ Jesus." In Matthew 11:28-30 Jesus says "Come to me, all who labour and are heavy laden, and I will give you rest. Take my yoke upon you, and learn from me, for I am gentle and lowly in heart, and you will find rest for your souls. For my yoke is easy, and my burden is light."

The human brain consists of sixty per cent fat. Fatty acids are amongst the most crucial molecules that determine the brain's integrity and ability to perform well. These essential fatty acids cannot be synthesized by the body and must be obtained from our diet. An unbalanced dietary intake of fatty acids is related to impaired brain function and disease.

The most common foods containing essential fatty acids are:

- fatty fish (especially salmon, herring, mackerel, and sardines),
- organic eggs,
- nuts (especially walnuts),
- seeds,
- avocados,
- vegetable oils (olive, sesame, avocado),
- seaweed and algae.

Other superfoods for a healthy brain are:

- fresh blueberries,
- fresh cherries,
- broccoli,
- kidney beans,
- coconut oil,
- turmeric,
- dark chocolate with little to no unhealthy sugars,
- honey and rice malt syrup as a substitute for sugar,
- leafy greens,
- celery,
- and beetroot.

Oxygen for the brain comes through normal breathing and exercise. Stress, inactivity, and pollution cause shallow breathing, whereas we are supposed to breathe deeply so that oxygen can reach the lower parts of our lungs. Shallow breathing due to lack of exercise causes us to lose some lung function. We become more fatigued as a result of the reduced oxygen to the blood and reduced circulation. Oxygen starvation leads to premature ageing, reduced vitality, a weaker immune system, sleeping disorders, anxiety, stomach upsets, heartburn, gas, muscle cramps, dizziness, visual problems, chest pain, heart palpitations, and all kinds of diseases including cancer.

When we don't have sufficient oxygen and we aren't expelling enough carbon dioxide, there is a build-up of toxins in every cell of our body. With a shallow breathing lifestyle, we use only about a tenth of our lung capacity. It is enough to survive, but not enough for a high quality of life and a high resistance to disease. When you inhale, push your stomach forward gently, and breathe through as though you are filling your stomach. This is called abdominal breathing. Then exhale slowly and gently, allowing your stomach to return to its normal position. The healthiest way of breathing is through your nose because it has defence mechanisms that prevent impurities and excessively cold air from entering the body. It also can detect poisonous gases that could be harmful through smelling sensors. Bacteria and viruses can enter the lungs through mouth breathing, so keep your mouth closed and let your nose do the work.

A study by senior author Jay Gottfried, Professor of Neurology at Feinberg was published on the 6th December 2016 in the Journal of Neuroscience. The finding was that the rhythm of breathing creates electrical activity in the human brain that enhances emotional judgments and memory recall. Researchers at Trinity College Institute of Neuroscience and the Global Brain Health Institute also found that focused breathing affects levels of noradrenaline, a natural brain chemical messenger. Noradrenaline gets released into the bloodstream when you are curious, focused, or emotionally aroused. It enhances your attention to detail and improves overall brain health by promoting the growth of new neural connections. In the brain, neurons connect to each other to form neural networks. Neurons are electrically excitable nerve cells and nerve fibres which process and transmit information. The brain is what it is because of the structural and functional properties of interconnected neurons. Oxygen plays a major part in all brain functions. The brain consumes roughly twenty per cent of the body's oxygen, which is enough to operate five to ten per cent of neurons at a time.

We must also include anti-oxidants in our diet, which help protect the cells in our brain and body from the damaging effects of highly reactive molecules called free radicals. The body is under constant attack from oxidative stress. This means that oxygen in the body splits into single atoms with unpaired electrons. These atoms are also called free radicals, and they like to be in pairs. They then scavenge the body to seek out other electrons so they can become a pair. Free radicals then try to fill their missing slot by stealing an electron from a nearby molecule. This starts a chain reaction, as the deprived molecules try to grab electrons from their neighbours, who in turn try to grab electrons from their neighbours, destabilizing them and turning them into free radicals. This process is called oxidation and is chemically the same process whereby oxygen rusts iron and turns a peeled apple brown. It causes damage to cells, proteins, and DNA.

Oxidative stress occurs when there are too many free radicals and too much cellular damage. Although free radicals are a crucial part of the immune system, floating through the veins and attacking foreign invaders, they also pose a danger to the body if there are too many. The overproduction of free radicals eventually leads to many chronic diseases such as atherosclerosis, cancer, diabetes, rheumatoid arthritis, post-ischemic perfusion injury, heart attacks, cardiovascular disease, chronic inflammation, stroke and septic shock, ageing and other degenerative diseases.

Anti-oxidants in our diet are substances which are helpful in defending against the effects of free radicals, either by breaking them into harmless substances, or by binding to them, and preventing them from attacking healthy cells. Vitamins A, C and E are anti-oxidant substances normally found in a healthy diet that includes lots of fruits like blueberries, cranberries, blackberries, prunes, strawberries, cherries, apples, and vegetables such as red beans, kidney beans, artichoke, black beans, russet potatoes (dark skin), fish oil, vegetable oils, nuts, dark chocolate, green tea, and green leafy vegetables. The hormone estrogen also has antioxidant properties.

Foods most harmful to the human body are sugar, gluten, and processed foods. They cause inflammation and are linked to all kinds of illnesses like diabetes, cancers, Parkinson's disease, asthma, depression, anxiety, and ADHD. These foods do not have any nutritional value and when we eat them every day we'll keep feeling hungry. We feel that we do not have energy and our bodies cannot function properly because we gave it the wrong fuel. It is like putting petrol in a diesel car which can cause serious damage to the fuel injection system and the engine. When the body does not receive the right foods, the brain keeps sending signals that we are hungry, and that is why we have the obesity problem today, as people do not know when they are full. Sugar creates havoc in the body. Some negative effects of eating sugar include: it makes us hungry so that we want to eat more; it interferes with our appetite hormones meaning that our body cannot tell when it is hungry or full; it prevents us from burning fat when we work out at the gym; it raises insulin; and as a result it programs our body to store more fat.

Consuming sugar in large amounts results in a burst of energy known as a 'sugar high', ending in a sharp drop in energy called a 'crash'. Artificial sweeteners on the other hand, work more like a pesticide in the body, and are stored as a toxin because they cannot be broken down. This causes diseases, kills the friendly bacteria in the gut, blocks oxygen from binding to red blood cells, blocks enzymes the body needs for normal function, blocks the absorption of vitamins and minerals, and interferes with DNA synthesis, attacking gut cells, and creating holes in the intestinal lining called 'leaky gut'.

So first we have to make sure that we feed our brain the right food and inhale enough clean oxygen to keep it healthy. Then we have to feed it with positive words and pictures to grow our knowledge and character. Ultimately this will help us build our confidence in life, resulting in a positive attitude that can easily connect with God and the Holy Spirit. Starting with reading and understanding God's words in the Bible is a huge step in helping to heal your body and mind. In Proverbs 4:20-22 God says "My son, pay attention to what I say; turn your ear to my words. Do not let them out of your sight, keep them within your heart; for they are life to those who find them and health to one's whole body." In this scripture 'your heart' refers to your mind.

Happiness follows when our brain and body is healthy. Secondly, is when we have decided to be happy. A person can think themselves happy or unhappy. Therefore when we feed our mind with happy thoughts, even in the midst of unhappiness, our mind will produce a happier life.

Clothed with Prosperity

Prosperity is defined as the state of flourishing, thriving, good fortune or successful social status. Prosperity often encompasses wealth but also includes other factors which can be independent of wealth, such as happiness and health.

With hard and clever work you can improve your financial status, but the only way for your finances to be protected from the thief of this world is to allow God to be in control of it. When you give God the reigns over your finances, He promises in Deuteronomy 28:12 that He will open to you His good treasury, and the heavens will give rain to your land in its season to bless all the work of your hands, and that you shall lend to many nations, but you shall not borrow. God wants to be your provider. 1 Chronicles 29:12 says all riches come from God and He rules over all.

What I have learned over the past few years is that because everything in this world belongs to God, including our finances, we cannot just buy whatever we want and enjoy life as we wish. To build our wealth, we must ask God before we spend money, left, right, and centre. When it comes to tithing and offerings, we must ask the Holy Spirit to show us who should receive our money, and how much. We have been made stewards of money by God. Understanding God's ownership changes how we look at money. We like to think of our money and possessions as ours, yet the Bible makes it very clear that God owns everything. Colossians 1:16 says that all things were created by Him and for Him, all things that are in heaven, and that are in the earth, visible and invisible, whether they be thrones, or dominions or principalities, or powers. Deuteronomy 10:14 also says "To the Lord your God belong the heavens, even the highest heavens, the earth and everything in it". So to give God control over our finances and everything we own, is the right thing to do. This will ensure that we will never have any shortage in our life, and we'll always be blessed if we have the right attitude about this.

We should remember never to measure our blessings with other brothers and sisters in Christ, because we all receive different blessings from God. The day you die you cannot take anything with you, so whatever is on earth belongs on earth, and whatever is in heaven belongs in heaven. Everything in this world goes through deterioration, even our physical bodies. In heaven, everything will live forever and ever, and there is no decay of any sort. There are no shortages in heaven, and Jesus will make sure you have everything you need. He promised us in John 14:2 "In my Father's house are many mansions: if it were not so, I would have told you. I go to prepare a place for you". So Jesus is preparing a place for everyone that gives their life to Him. He will look after you forever and all He asks is that you love Him and acknowledge Him for who He is, and who He says He is. Proverbs 3:6 says "In all thy ways acknowledge Him, and He shall direct thy paths".

Clothed with Knowledge and Wisdom

The only way to grow intellectually and in knowledge is to study, read a lot, attend seminars, and watch educational videos or movies. To be intellectually sound is all up to you, but make sure you have a filter on what you allow into your mind. For example, you cannot think it is alright to study the occult, watch pornographic videos or play violent video games, and not be affected by it.

In 2 Timothy 3:16 we read "All scripture is given by inspiration of God, and is profitable for doctrine, for reproof, for correction, for instruction in righteousness". So every word that God gave us in the Bible can be trusted. It was written over a span of 1500 years, by 40 writers who were inspired by the Holy Spirit. That is not to say it took 1500 years to write the Bible, only that it took that long for the complete canon of Scripture to be written as God progressively revealed His Word. Most scholars believe that either Genesis or Job is the oldest Bible book and was written by Moses around 1400 BC (before Christ). The newest book, Revelation was written around 90 AD (standing for **Anno Domini**, meaning in the year of the Lord or the year Jesus was born). Unlike other religious writings, the Bible reads like a factual news account of real events, places, and people. Historians and archaeologists have repeatedly confirmed its authenticity. Archaeologists have consistently discovered the names of government officials, kings, cities, and festivals mentioned in the Bible. Sometimes historians didn't think such people or places existed. For example, the Gospel of John tells of Jesus healing a cripple next to the Pool of Bethesda. The text even describes the five porticoes (walkways) leading to the pool. Scholars didn't think the pool existed, until archaeologists found it forty feet below the ground, complete with the five porticoes. (Strobel, Lee. The Case for Christ, Zondervan Publishing House, 1998, p. 132.)

Many of the ancient locations mentioned by Luke, in the Book of Acts in the New Testament, have been identified through archaeology.

"In all, Luke names thirty-two countries, fifty-four cities and nine islands without an error." (Geisler, Norman L. Baker Encyclopedia of Christian Apologetics, Grand Rapids: Baker, 1998). There are so many proofs that the Bible is indeed the Word of God that were written by different authors who were inspired by God's Spirit. There is no doubt in my mind that the Bible was written by God Himself for his people because I have studied and read a lot of history on this. If you are still not convinced, I suggest that you find trustworthy sources on the history and authenticity of the Bible. The proofs of the Bible and how it came into existence are really mind-blowing.

I know that when you start off reading the Bible it is not always easy to understand. Keep reading it anyway and ask the Holy Spirit to help you understand it. You can even join a Bible study group, who will help you understand the scriptures better. The sooner a person begins to understand the Bible, the sooner life will start making sense, and the sooner they will understand how to protect themselves from the evil in this world.

Wisdom is different from knowledge. Knowledge is about facts and ideas that we acquire through study, experience, observation, research, or investigation. Wisdom is the ability to discern and judge which aspects of that knowledge are true, right, lasting, and applicable to our life. One can be knowledgeable without being wise. Knowledge is to know how to use a gun; whereas wisdom is to know when to use it and when to keep it holstered. The book of Proverbs in the Bible is the best place to learn about biblical wisdom. Proverbs 1:7 speaks of both biblical knowledge and wisdom: "The fear of the LORD is the beginning of knowledge, but fools despise wisdom and instruction." The Wisdom of God is directly linked to the Holy Spirit. Only through the Holy Spirit can we gain the hidden wisdom of God and the Bible. Wisdom in God's ways is listed as one of the gifts of the Holy Spirit (1 Corinthians 12:8). To receive wisdom about God and the Bible, we have to study it first. Only then can the wisdom and hidden truths break through from the Holy Spirit. That is why it is important to keep reading the Bible even if we do not understand it all. There will be parts that we do understand and with time spent in the Word of God it will break through as we continue to study. If we want a blessed life that is connected to God, we have to make time to study His words and His ways, and not just rely on preachers and anointed people to teach us. God will teach us Himself through the Holy Spirit as we study the Bible. James 4:8 says that if we draw near to God, He will draw near to us.

I had a friend reading this book and when she got to this part she said when she was lost and had no knowledge of God, He spoke to her in an audible voice. Therefore she believed she received the wisdom from God before she had any knowledge of Him. This was an interesting point of view and I thought to investigate it a bit more. We can ask the following questions then: What happens to a person when God suddenly reveals Himself by speaking or appearing to them, and then they start speaking in tongues? Does this mean they received wisdom from God?

A beautiful moment like this where God makes Himself known to a person who did not know of Him before is called a 'supernatural encounter with God'. Not all people will encounter God in such a powerful way. Indeed when God reveals Himself, there will be some Godly wisdom that is deposited in that moment. If that person does not want to pursue God after such an encounter, I do not think that person will stay wise. The Bible is full of scriptures promising us that if we seek God wholeheartedly, we will find Him. The closer we draw to God, the more we'll hear the Holy Spirit's voice, and the voices coming from the world will move more to the background. That is what this friend of mine did. She started going to church, and wanted to learn more about the person who talked to her and called himself God.

Wisdom is to become consciously aware of your subconscious mind. Knowledge is what we read, study, and what we can see. Whereas wisdom is that sixth sense. One day I was watching a testimony of an American Christian Actor, on Christian television, who was looking to see if he could find underground water on his land. He booked a drilling company who had drilled for water twice before, and could not find any. It cost him a lot of money for those two drilling sessions. Then he decided he was not going to give up and asked them to come back a third time. Before they started to drill again, he asked them where they thought could be water. When they showed him the spot, he said to go ahead and drill. They'd drilled deeper than they normally would have, and did not find water. He asked them to continue. They got to a point where they had to make a decision to stop. The actor had such great hopes because he felt in his spirit that he would find water on his land. He asked the drilling company if they could drill a bit further, and if they do not find water, they could stop. Only four inches deeper delivered a huge underwater river. This is how wisdom works that we receive from the Holy Spirit. It works against all worldly rules. The actor kept listening to that inner voice, which must have been the Holy Spirit, and he did not give up. If he did not ask to go that extra bit further, he would have missed this huge blessing from God.

When a person suddenly speaks in tongues it is the presence of God (The Holy Spirit) that causes the person to speak in a heavenly language, which only God can understand, and those whom God gives interpretation to. To me it shows that God Himself intervenes for His beloved child to turn his or her life around for the better. Some people believe there are two kinds of wisdom, worldly wisdom, and Godly wisdom. After reading a few people's views on these two wisdoms, I came to the conclusion there is no such thing as worldly wisdom. Wisdom is wisdom and can only come from God. Let's take the example of earlier where I said knowledge is to know how to use a gun, whereas wisdom is to know when to use it, and when to keep it holstered. One of the Ten Commandments that God gave to Moses for the Israelites in Exodus 20 is "You shall not murder". Therefore this is a commandment or law from God not to kill another person. If you know this law and accepted Jesus as your Lord, the Holy Spirit will keep you on the straight and narrow. This wisdom will make a person feeling guilty when they want to take another person's life.

Clothed with the Armour of God

Our spiritual protection also comes from God. In 2 Thessalonians 3:3 we read that the Lord is faithful, and he will strengthen us and protect us from the evil one, which is the devil.

Protection against harm from the devil and his demons, and from our enemies, is one of the ways that God shows His love towards His children, that is everyone who believes in God the Father, Jesus Christ the Son, and the Holy Spirit. Thank God that a young child, who cannot yet understand or reason, belongs to Him. According to the Bible, God does allow trials in our life for His own special purpose. Trials are used to draw us near to Him, to help us grow, or to protect us from even bigger harm. The good news is that He promises in 1 Corinthians 10:13 that He is faithful and will not let us be tempted beyond what we can bear. If you are going through a trial right now, take refuge in Him, as He is our secret hiding place. Pray and fast to attract His divine protection. No matter how bad your situation may look, always trust in the Lord. Nahum 1:7 says "The Lord is good, a refuge in times of trouble. He cares for those who trust in Him." The Lord declares in Isaiah 54:17 "No weapon formed against you shall prosper; and every tongue which rises against you in judgment He shall condemn. This is the heritage of the servants of the Lord, and their righteousness is from Him".

Things you can do to secure God's divine protection for yourself and your family:

- Accept Jesus Christ as your Lord and Saviour.
- Love God the Father, Jesus Christ, and the Holy Spirit with all of your heart.

- Do not grieve the Holy Spirit by denying His existence and not allowing Him to lead you. Other things that grieve the Holy Spirit are, corrupting talk, bitterness, slander, malice, and anger (Ephesians 4:29-32).
- Pray daily – morning and night. Also pray as a family together.
- Read the Bible daily. Make it a mission to read it from beginning to end.
- Display Bible Verses of protection all over your house, inside and out, through ornaments, paintings, stickers, books, painted rocks.
- Play Christian music in your house daily.
- Have regular communion to celebrate what Jesus has done for you on the cross.
- Watch and listen to Godly inspired sermons, talk shows, and motivational speakers.
- Put on the armour of God daily by saying it out loud and living it out.

The Armour of God is found in Ephesians 6:10-18:

"10. Finally, be strong in the Lord and in His mighty power.
11. Put on the full armour of God, so that you can take your stand against the devil's schemes.
12. For our struggle is not against flesh and blood, but against the rulers, against the authorities, against the powers of this dark world and against the spiritual forces of evil in the heavenly realms.
13. Therefore put on the full armour of God, so that when the day of evil comes, you may be able to stand your ground, and after you have done everything, to stand.
14. Stand firm then, with the *belt of truth* buckled around your waist, with the *breastplate of righteousness* in place,
15. and with your *feet fitted with the readiness* that comes *from the gospel of peace.*
16. In addition to all this, take up the *shield of faith*, with which you can extinguish all the flaming arrows of the evil one.

17. Take the *helmet of salvation* and the *sword of the Spirit*, which is the Word of God.
18. And *pray in the Spirit* on all occasions with all kinds of prayers and requests. With this in mind, be alert and always keep on praying for all the Lord's people."

How do you live your life clothed with the full Armour of God?

The *belt of truth* is to live and walk in the truth in all your ways. Do not lie or cheat! A lie, no matter how small, gives an open door for the devil and his demons to attack you. The truth chases them far away. The Bible describes the devil as the father of all lies. John 8:44 says "You belong to your father, the devil, and you want to carry out your father's desires. He was a murderer from the beginning, not holding to the truth, for there is no truth in him. When he lies, he speaks his native language, for he is a liar and the father of lies."

The *breastplate of righteousness* means to live an honourable and ethical life – one of integrity, and goodness, being blameless, and sinless. Righteousness is the perfect holiness of Christ and is an essential attribute to the character of God. It means to be someone who chooses what is right and it is the opposite of sin. When the devil comes for you, he has no hold over you if you are righteous. We cannot become righteous through our own good works, but only through accepting Jesus and the Holy Spirit into our heart. Through them we become righteous.

Fit your feet with shoes of gospel and peace means that you are ready and willing to spread the gospel of peace that Jesus came to teach people while He was on earth during His 'First Coming'. His teachings contain the Good News of what His crucifixion accomplished for us and can be understood by reading the four Gospel Books at the beginning of the New Testament.

The *shield of faith* is an important piece in any battle of war. A shield is used to fend off arrows, spears, and swords. So when the devil shoots his arrows of doubt, lies, unbelief, accusations etc, we can defend ourselves with the shield of faith. Faith comes by hearing and hearing by the Word of God. Through studying the Bible, we'll recognize the arrows from the devil and defend ourselves with God's words and truths.

The *helmet of salvation* protects our mind. It is protected because of what Jesus has given us by His death and resurrection. In 1 Corinthians 2:14-16 we read "The natural person does not accept the things of the Spirit of God, for they are folly to him, and he is not able to understand them because they are spiritually discerned. The spiritual person judges all things but is himself to be judged by no one. For who has understood the mind of the Lord so as to instruct him? But we have the mind of Christ." Accepting and believing what Jesus accomplished for us by His death and resurrection gives us the assurance that we are saved.

The *sword of the Spirit* represents the Word of God. A sword is a weapon which can be used to attack and kill. Hebrews 4:12 says "For the Word of God is alive and active. Sharper than any double-edged sword, it penetrates even to dividing soul and spirit, joints and marrow; it judges the thoughts and attitudes of the heart." So when we know the Bible well, we can attack the devil with the scriptures, and he will flee from us. He'll think twice before he comes back to attack us when he recognizes that we know God's Word well.

Pray in the Spirit means to pray in tongues where the Holy Spirit communicates to God through you, for you and others. Praying in tongues is the strongest form of prayer because the devil and his demons do not understand what is prayed. Any form of prayer with meaning and surrender to God is powerful. The devil hates it when we pray because he knows that prayer strengthens us and keeps us alert to his deception.

Clothed with Style and Beauty

For too long the misconception has existed that to make oneself look good and beautiful is evil, as God only looks on the inside and not to our outer appearance. For many years this belief was deeply ingrained into my own soul. Maybe it came from our childhood when we were insecure, and family and people who cared about our mental well-being were saying that what is in our heart makes the difference to who we really are. People who care about us will say this to protect us from thoughts that we are ugly and not good enough. Of course, it is not wrong to say that what is in your heart defines who you are! I believe that the state of a person's heart (mind) is one of the deciding factors as to whether they are going to heaven or hell when departing from this earth. Mark 7:21-23 says "For it is from within, out of a person's heart, that evil thoughts come - sexual immorality, theft, murder, adultery, greed, malice, deceit, lewdness, envy, slander, arrogance and folly. All these evils come from inside and defile a person."

We must always dress with style and respect for God, for ourselves and for the people around us. Women especially need to take note of the neckline and hemline of a garment. Too many women expose their bodies to the world in a disrespectful manner. I am not suggesting you hide under layers of material either. When you read my book *Style Yourself with Confidence* you'll realise our aim should be to dress stylishly rather than fashionably.

God sent Prophet Samuel to Jesse to anoint one of his sons as the future King of Judah. In 1 Samuel 16:7 the Lord said to Samuel, "Do not consider his appearance or his height, for I have rejected him. The Lord does not look at the things people look at. People look at the outward appearance, but the Lord looks at the heart." Here God refers to the stature and height of the future king of Judah first and then He refers to a good heart. God was preparing Samuel beforehand so that he would know that the son he was about to anoint as king was of smaller stature than the rest of his brothers. Three of Jesse's oldest sons followed Saul to war. These three sons would have been well-built. Seven sons appeared in front of Samuel but he said to Jesse, "The Lord has not chosen these." and he asked, "Are these all the sons you have?" Jesse said that his youngest son, David, was tending the sheep. Samuel sends for David to be brought in front of him. When David arrived he was glowing with *health* and had a *fine appearance and handsome features*. Then the Lord said, "Rise and anoint him; this is the one." In 1 Samuel 16:12, I could see that David's healthy appearance and handsome features were pleasing to God. By reading the period of King David's reign, you'll notice a few times where he was referred to as 'a man after God's own heart', not only because of his appearance but also because of his good and righteous heart.

There are many Bible verses telling us that the inner beauty of a gentle and quiet spirit is worth much to God, but it does not mean that we have to neglect our appearance. King David's song of praise to God says in Psalm 139:14 "I praise You because I am fearfully and wonderfully made; Your works are wonderful, I know that full well." Do not forget that God created mankind in His own image and likeness. After God finished creating the earth and everything in it, including mankind, we read in Genesis 1:31 that God saw all that he had made, and it was very good.

When I first heard God calling me to help build His people's confidence through coaching them on their outer appearance, I was a bit worried about how I would do it because we are all so conditioned to thinking that beauty is the last thing we should worry about. In Ezekiel 16:10-15 God said the following about the people in the city, Jerusalem "I clothed you with an embroidered dress and put sandals of fine leather on you. I dressed you in fine linen and covered you with costly garments. I adorned you with jewellery: I put bracelets on your arms and a necklace around your neck, and I put a ring on your nose, earrings on your ears and a beautiful crown on your head.

So you were adorned with gold and silver; your clothes were of fine linen and costly fabric and embroidered cloth. Your food was honey, olive oil, and the finest flour. You became very beautiful and rose to be a queen. And your fame spread among the nations on account of your beauty, because the splendour I had given you made your beauty perfect, declares the Sovereign Lord. But you trusted in your beauty and used your fame to become a prostitute. You lavished your favours on anyone who passed by and your beauty became his."

As I was reading through the Bible I realised that beauty is only evil when it is used for evil. The book of Ezekiel chapters 23 and 24 describe the lives of two adulterous sisters who were beautiful but who engaged in prostitution from a young age, and became worse as their lives continued. Although these two sisters' lives were used by God as examples to portray the spiritual infidelity of the two nations, Israel and Judah, it is also a story showing us how people, especially women, can use the beauty God has given them for the wrong cause. God's children were not created for the world, but for Him, and to glorify Him alone. God wants us to be beautiful and well cared for, for Him. He is the King, and our bodies are the temple of His indwelling Holy Spirit, therefore we must represent Him well on this earth. Read more in Chapter 4 of this book about why our countenance and appearance are important to the Lord.

Clothed with Humility

In 1 Peter 5:5-6 we read: "Likewise you younger people, submit yourselves to your elders. Yes, all of you be submissive to one another, and be clothed with humility, for God resists the proud, but gives grace to the humble. Therefore humble yourselves under the mighty hand of God, that He may exalt you in due time."

Have you seen the formula in this scripture? God says to be submissive to one another and to humble yourselves under God, and He will exalt you at the right time. The New Testament is full of blessings for those who put others before themselves.

How do you submit yourself to others?

- By being grateful for who you are and what you have.
- Not being in competition with others.
- Not comparing yourself to others.
- Spending more time listening to and encouraging others rather than talking about, or praising yourself.
- Complimenting others to help build their confidence.
- By helping people who are in need.
- Being the first to say sorry or admit when you are wrong.
- Enter last into a door or room.
- Taking the smallest piece of cake or meal.
- Always being fair and righteous in everything you do.
- Living in peace and unity with others.
- Standing up for the oppressed.
- Showing love and understanding at all times.
- Not being self-centred. Ask Jesus every day what you can do for Him to make this world a better place, rather than always asking Him what you want.

Romans 12:16 says "Live in harmony with one another. Do not be proud, but be willing to associate with people of low position. Do not be conceited."

How do you humble yourself before God? By admitting that you are a sinner, and that you need His forgiveness, knowing that there is no way that you can go to heaven and live in eternity without the sacrifice that Jesus Christ made for you on the cross. Realise that you belong to Christ, and not to yourself. Ask Jesus how you can live your life to glorify Him, looking forward to the day you will be reunited with Him. Give your life to Jesus and ask Him to show you what your assignment is here on earth. Even James 4:10 says: "Humble yourselves in the sight of the Lord, and He will lift you up."

Humility does not mean we must be silent or passive! We must spread the Good News and testify in love to all the people that God sends on our path, and when we get a prompting from the Holy Spirit. Never use force to sway other's opinion to your way of thinking. Live your life in love and humility. This is the best approach to win souls for the Kingdom of God.

Jesus came in humility to earth to be crucified for our sins and transgressions. When He comes back to judge this world, He will come in all His Glory as the King of kings. Every knee shall bow, and every tongue shall confess that Jesus Christ is Lord (Romans 14:11).

Jesus is God who was Clothed with Humanity

Jesus Christ, who is God, became flesh and lived among His people on earth for thirty-three years. In other words, He was born with a human body that He helped to create in the beginning. In humility, He served His people by dying on the cross in their place and rising again to give them eternal life. Jesus stepped down from His throne in heaven to be clothed with humanity for the purpose of salvation for all who believe in Him. No other god can offer what we have received from Jesus Christ our Creator, Saviour, and Lord.

Christianity is a religion based on Jesus Christ and His teachings in the Bible. Jesus never called his followers Christians, nor did the early Church call themselves Christians. The name 'Christian' was created by people outside the church to describe those who accepted, believed, and followed Jesus Christ. Many people describe themselves as Christians today but not all are true followers of Jesus. Even Jesus himself said in Matthew 7:21 "Not everyone who says to Me, 'Lord, Lord,' shall enter the kingdom of heaven, but he who does the will of My Father in heaven."

True followers of Jesus are not just hearers of the words of God in the Bible, but are doers of what God teaches. Christians are not a special group of people who are secured to go to heaven and live in eternity. We must first believe in Jesus Christ and that He is who He says He is, the Son of God who died for our sins on the cross. Secondly, we must come to a point where we love God and Jesus with all of our heart, and give our life to them. An outward sign or confirmation is water baptism, which is explained in chapter 3. The inward confirmation comes from the Holy Spirit. Thirdly, and very important, is to have an intimate relationship with Jesus through talking to Him daily, listening and recognizing His voice, and very importantly, reading and studying the Bible regularly to get equipped in God's ways, teachings, and guidance. Jesus, with the help of the Holy Spirit, will testify for you on *Judgment Day*, and will reward you with eternal life. Therefore Jesus wants to know you personally through your communication with Him in prayer.

CHAPTER 2

There is NO Greater Love Than This!

> "For God so loved the world, that He gave His only Son (Jesus), that whoever believes in Him should not perish but have eternal life" - John 3:16

This is how easy it is to live eternally with our God and Creator in heaven after we have passed away from this earth. Believing that Jesus Christ is the Son of God, who came to earth as a man to be crucified, and rise again, paying the ultimate price for sin forever. The Bible says in Romans 10:9 that if we confess with our mouth, 'Jesus is Lord', and believe in our heart that God raised Him from the dead, we will be saved. There is nothing more to be done to wipe out the sin that started with Adam and Eve in the Garden of Eden. We cannot earn salvation; God's grace saves us from eternal death. Confessing with your mouth means that you must declare it out aloud.

In Romans 5:8 we read that God demonstrates His own love towards us, in that while we were yet sinners, Christ died for us. God's brilliant plan has voided the devil's plan to corrupt His children forever. The good news is that everybody on this earth can be saved and can go to heaven when they die. The sad fact is, that not all people accept this free gift, as they do not believe in Jesus Christ and what He has accomplished for them.

Why does the devil want to keep corrupting God's children?

God created a powerful, intelligent and beautiful angelic being that was a chief angel in heaven called Lucifer (meaning 'bearer of light' or 'morning star'). Lucifer was established by God to be the angel of worship, whose ministry surrounded the heart of heaven. Ezekiel 28:13 says "Thou hast been in Eden the garden of God; every precious stone was thy covering, the sardius, topaz, and the diamond, the beryl, the onyx, and the jasper, the sapphire, the emerald, and the carbuncle, and gold: the workmanship of thy tabrets and of thy pipes was prepared in thee in the day that thou wast created." He was also created to dwell eternally in the throne room of heaven, in the very presence of God (Ezekiel 28:14). To dwell in the presence of a perfect God, Lucifer had to be perfect. From the day he was created he was blameless in his ways until wickedness was found in him (Ezekiel 28:15). Lucifer was made very good according to the scriptures. He was also given free choice, and could choose between good and evil, just as Adam and Eve could, but he became so impressed with his own beauty, intelligence, power, and position that he began to desire for himself the honour and glory that belonged to God alone. Ezekiel 28:17 describes why Lucifer was expelled from heaven "Your heart became proud on account of your beauty, and you corrupted your wisdom because of your splendour. So I threw you to the earth; I made a spectacle of you before kings". The sin that corrupted Lucifer was self-generated pride. He wanted to be worshipped like God, but God does not share His glory, nor does He permit another to receive worship due to him. As a result, Lucifer was banished from heaven, and his name has changed from Lucifer meaning 'morning star' to Satan meaning 'adversary'. Other names in the Bible that Satan is known by are Devil, Beelzebub, Mephistopheles, Antichrist, Belial, Dragon, Enemy, Liar, Power of darkness, Roaring lion, Serpent, Ruler of this world, Murderer, Thief, Tempter, Wicked one, Accuser, Adversary. There are many more names that you will find as you read through the Bible.

In Isaiah 14:12-15 we read how Lucifer fell from heaven "How you have fallen from heaven, morning star, son of the dawn! You have been cast down to the earth, you who once laid low the nations! You said in your heart, "I will ascend to the heavens; I will raise my throne above the stars of God; I will sit enthroned on the mount of assembly, on the utmost heights of Mount Zaphon. I will ascend above the tops of the clouds; I will make myself like the Most High. But you are brought down to the realm of the dead, to the depths of the pit." Revelation 12:4 gives us some indication of how many angels Lucifer corrupted that were also banished from heaven "Its tail swept a third of the stars out of the sky and flung them to the earth....."

Satan hates the human race that was created by God in His own image. He hates you because God loves you so much. Every time he sees you, it reminds him that he can never be like you. You have the power to crush his head through Jesus Christ. In Genesis 3:15 God said to the serpent, He will put enmity between him (the devil) and the woman, and between his offspring (spiritual descendants or followers) and hers (Jesus); Jesus will crush his head, and the devil will strike His heel.

Satan is so happy if people do not believe that he exists because that means he can work undetected in their lives. What most people do when things go wrong is to blame God, not recognizing the work of Satan. Sadly there are many people who become Satan worshippers willingly through recruitment either by Satan himself, or by other Satan worshippers. They infiltrate the lives of children and young adults very subtle. When they are in too deep they find it hard to escape this dark and evil world. A great book to read on how Satan can come into your life is a book written by John Ramirez called *Unmasking the Devil.* John was a high ranking devil worshipper for over two decades, until he was saved by Jesus Christ, and is now teaching God's children how the devil operates so that they can avoid the traps. The amazing news is that when an adult or child repents of their sins, giving their lives to our Lord Jesus Christ, He will help them to get out of the clutches of the devil and his demons.

After Lucifer was stripped of his glory and name of 'morning star', it was given to a far more deserving individual, the Son of God. In Revelation 22:16 Jesus Christ is called the 'Bright and Morning Star'. Today, Jesus is seated at the right hand of God, dwelling in the presence of the Almighty One.

Do not deny your free gift in Jesus Christ from God the Father!

Hell was created by God for the devil and his fallen angels, who rebelled against Him. It is not enough for the devil to take his punishment to burn in hell forever. He tries to cause as many of God's children as he can, to also rebel against God their Creator. Because God is Love, and He loves all His children, the devil tries to hurt God by turning His children against Him. Now that you know this, do not allow the devil to steal God's free gift of eternal life from you. You are given the choice of going to heaven or hell after you die. What will you choose? I choose heaven, and I hope you do too! There are around a hundred Bible verses telling us that there is only one way to receive eternal life. John 3:36 is a clear message saying whoever believes in the Son has eternal life; whoever does not obey the Son shall not see life, but the wrath of God remains on him.

Study the Bible to learn all His commands, and follow His guidance to have a blessed life that can start while you are on earth.

In Hosea 4:6 God says that His people are destroyed for lack of knowledge. The more you know about God's words and laws in the Bible, the quicker you will recognize when the devil tries to enter your life.

Do's and Don'ts for a Prosperous Life

1. Blessed is the man: Who walks not in the counsel of the ungodly, Nor stands in the path of sinners, Nor sits in the seat of the scornful;

2. But his delight is in the law of the Lord, And in His law he meditates day and night.

3. He shall be like a tree planted by the rivers of water, That brings forth its fruit in its season, Whose leaf also shall not wither; And whatever he does shall prosper. (Psalm 1:1-3)

CHAPTER 3

We Belong to the King!

> "Or do you not know that your body is the temple of the Holy Spirit who is in you, whom you have from God, and you are not your own? For you were bought at a price; therefore glorify God in your body and in your spirit, which are God's." - 1 Corinthians 6:19

If you really love God as much as He loves you, you will understand that you were bought at a price. Jesus' blood, that was shed on the cross for you, was the price paid for your salvation and inheritance to be a son or daughter of God the Father. Galatians 3:26 says that in Christ Jesus we are all children of God through faith. Everyone accepting this gift does not belong to themselves anymore, but to Jesus who paid the price.

When sin came into this world in the Garden of Eden, our relationship with God was destroyed. Because He is so holy, sin could not come into His presence. Therefore God's people on earth could not talk to God the Father freely, and face-to-face as Adam and Eve could in the beginning. Thankfully through the cross, Jesus repaired our relationship with God the Father.

Through His indwelling Spirit, we have direct communication with God the Father again, so that our relationship is restored, just as in Adam and Eve's time. The added benefit we have today compared to the Garden of Eden is that we now know how the devil operates. He is exposed through the Word of God, and we can easily recognize him and his works so that we can resist him. We have a much better covenant than the first man and woman ever had, through Jesus Christ. The devil has many tricks up his sleeve and here are a few obvious ones to recognize him. These are:

- Not believing in Almighty God (that is God the Father, God the Son - Jesus Christ, and God the Holy Spirit).
- Not believing that Jesus Christ died and rose for our sins.
- Having doubt and fear.
- Not trusting God to look after us.
- Unhappiness.
- Pride.
- Lust.
- The hunger for power.
- The love of money.
- Hatred.
- Anger and bitterness.
- Jealousy.
- Unforgiveness.
- Discouragement.
- The love of pleasure.
- Selfishness.
- Anxiety.
- Addictions.
- Mismanagement of the finances God entrusted us with.
- Not believing in the devil.
- Not believing there is a hell.

If it was not for Jesus who died and rose again for us, we would all perish. Because of the cross and his victory over death, we can live forever, but only if we decide to accept God's gift to us. The fact that Jesus died for all, means we belong to Him. 1 Corinthians 3:23 says "and you belong to Christ, and Christ belongs to God." By giving your life to the Lord, you received the following privileges.

1. All your sins are forgiven.

The main purpose of Jesus crucifixion was to wash you clean from all your sins because through the cross he has taken every sin and illness of this world on Him forever. There is no more price to pay for the sins of this world. It was done once for all who lived before, those who are still living, and those who will be born in the future. How wonderful is that! Hebrew 10:10 confirms this "…we have been made holy through the sacrifice of the body of Jesus Christ once for all."

2. You'll live forever and will never die.

In John 10:28-30 Jesus says "I give them eternal life, and they shall never perish; no one will snatch them out of my hand. My Father, who has given them to me, is greater than all; no one can snatch them out of my Father's hand. I and the Father are one." Therefore when you die here on earth, you'll continue your afterlife in heaven forever with God the Father, Jesus Christ the Son, and the Holy Spirit.

3. Your direct communication to God the Father and Jesus Christ is restored.

You can talk to them and they will talk to you in the following ways: Through the Holy Spirit living within you, or by Jesus appearing to you face-to-face. God and Jesus sometimes talk through an audible voice close to you. It can be through thoughts and dreams. When reading the Bible, God will speak to you through different scriptures. One can also sense or feel God's presence without seeing or hearing Him. God will sometimes use other believers to bring His messages to you.

Jesus says in John 10:27 "My sheep hear my voice; I know them and they follow me." Jesus identifies Himself in this verse as the Shepherd, and we are His sheep. Sheep follow their shepherd, and that is how Jesus wants us to follow his voice. He sees and knows the past, present, and future. We will be much better off by trusting Him and following his voice that teaches, protects, guides, and warns against any danger.

4. You have received power from the Holy Spirit

All children of God who accept Jesus Christ as their Lord and Saviour, and who have been born again, receive the Holy Spirit. His power is so powerful, that it raised Christ from the dead after His crucifixion. Romans 8:11 says "And if the Spirit of Him who raised Jesus from the dead lives in you, He who raised Christ from the dead will also give life to your mortal bodies because of His Spirit who lives in you."

5. Jesus promised that He will always look after you.

In Matthew 6:25-34 He says "Therefore I tell you, do not be anxious about your life, what you will eat or what you will drink, nor about your body, what you will put on. Is not life more than food, and the body more than clothing? Look at the birds of the air: they neither sow nor reap nor gather into barns, and yet your heavenly Father feeds them. Are you not of more value than they? And which of you by being anxious can add a single hour to his span of life? And why are you anxious about clothing? Consider the lilies of the field, how they grow: they neither toil nor spin, yet I tell you, even Solomon in all his glory was not arrayed like one of these. But if God so clothes the grass of the field, which today is alive and tomorrow is thrown into the oven, will He not much more clothe you, O you of little faith? Therefore do not be anxious, saying, 'What shall we eat?' or 'What shall we drink?' or 'What shall we wear?' For the Gentiles seek after all these things, and your heavenly Father knows that you need them all. But seek first the kingdom of God and His righteousness, and all these things will be added to you. Therefore do not be anxious about tomorrow, for tomorrow will be anxious for itself. Sufficient for the day is its own trouble."

Jesus does not just want to look after you, He also wants to prosper you! Some Christians think that it is unholy to ask to be financially blessed. This is so far from the truth. Jesus wants you to have more than enough. In Proverbs 8:17, 18, 21 God says "17. I love those who love Me, and those who seek Me find Me. 18. With me are riches and honour, enduring wealth and prosperity. 21. bestowing a rich inheritance on those who love me and making their treasuries full."

6. Through His stripes, we are healed physically and mentally.

God wants His people well. To walk in your right and inheritance of being healthy, you've got to make the Word of God first place and final authority in your life. Isaiah 53:5 reads "But He was wounded for our transgressions, He was bruised for our iniquities; The chastisement for our peace was upon Him, *And by His stripes, we are healed.*" We also have to do our part by looking after our body the best we can. My book *How to Look and Feel Younger for Longer* goes into more detail.

7. Jesus promised to protect you.

The Lord promised us that He is faithful, and He will strengthen you and protect you from the evil one (2 Thessalonians 3:3). When

God allows trials in our lives it is usually to draw us closer to Him or to test us on how we will handle it. Trials are also used to make us become a better person, and when we understand pain and suffering, we can support our family and fellow brothers and sisters to help make their trials easier. He is faithful and will not let us be tempted beyond what we can bear. If you are going through a trial right now, take refuge in Him, as He is our secret hiding place. In all your trials, trust in the Lord and give the problems to Him, so that He can guide you through. Praying and fasting will attract His divine protection during difficult times.

8. *Jesus will make known to you future revelations.*

In the Old Testament God regularly revealed mysteries to some of His children, and kings, and prophets. He revealed the future and His will to Moses; In Genesis 17:4 He revealed to Abraham that he would be the father of many nations. He revealed to King Nebuchadnezzar what will take place in the latter days; God warned Noah about the big flood that was coming, and instructed him to build the ark to protect his family, and preserve samples of all animals and birds; The Lord appeared to Samuel and made known to him what would happen in the future. Daniel received mysteries and revelations of the future; In Jeremiah 33:3 God said to Prophet Jeremiah "Ask me and I will tell you remarkable secrets you do not know, about things to come"; The Angel Gabriel was sent to John the Baptist's father, Zechariah, to reveal to him that his wife Elizabeth, who had always been barren, would give birth to a son, and the son's name should be John; The Angel Gabriel also appeared to the Virgin Mary, and told her that she would give birth to a son and that she should call him Jesus because He would save His people from their sins; The Prophet Isaiah predicted that Jesus would be the Messiah; and many more!

God is still communicating and revealing the future to His people today and will do it forever! In Hebrews 13:8 we read that

Jesus Christ is the same yesterday, today, and forever. Jesus states in John 16:14 that He will make mysteries known to you through the Holy Spirit. This same Spirit of God came upon the Apostles ten days after the ascension of our Lord Jesus into heaven, and the Holy Spirit has been here on earth ever since.

9. We are God's stewards and managers over all the good things He created.

God created human beings in His image, to be above all other creatures on earth. We have dominion over all living creatures. When God created mankind He said, "Let us make mankind in our image, in our likeness, so that they may rule over the fish in the sea and the birds in the sky, over the livestock and all the wild animals, and over all the creatures that move along the ground."

The first command that God gave his people was to fill the earth and cultivate the land. Genesis 1:28-29 God blessed them and said to them, "Be fruitful and increase in number; fill the earth and subdue it. Rule over the fish in the sea and the birds in the sky and over every living creature that moves on the ground". Then God said "I give you every seed-bearing plant on the face of the whole earth and every tree that has fruit with seed in it. They will be yours for food".

King David wrote in Psalm 8:4-5 "what is mankind that You are mindful of them, human beings that you care for them? You have made them a little lower than the angels and crowned them with glory and honour." What an awesome privilege and honour that God has entrusted us to care for His creation. This does not mean that we can do anything we want with it, without thinking of the consequences. Unfortunately, through human greed, people are destroying God's creation and are damaging the lives of others. As children of God, we have a responsibility to care about what happens to the earth and the people on it. Our responsibility is to ensure that the world can sustain all of God's people and animals.

The Feeling of Belonging

Every child and adult wants to feel they belong to a family. Children growing up without their parents or with only one of their parents, usually feel a void in their lives. No matter who we are, we need to have a sense of belonging. God created us as a family that belongs together. The Psalmist of Psalm 139, King David, wrote in verse 13 "For You (God) formed my inward parts; You knitted me together in my mother's womb". The unloving and not-belonging feelings often start in people's younger years when parents are absent from their lives. This can be due to death, adoption, separation, divorce or neglect. Because of this empty feeling, people and children will try to find love and a sense of belonging in the wrong places, and with the wrong crowds.

When a child grows up in a loving home with a parent or parents teaching them the truths of the Bible, and how they first belong to God before they belong to their parents, will create a sense of belonging. This sense gives inner confidence, and will produce a happier life, so no matter what, your first parent figure in life should be God the Father. As parents, we have a duty to teach our children this truth. When they know that their 'Parent', so to speak, is God first, I believe a lot of the issues with children around the world would improve and even disappear. We need to teach them how to communicate with their Father in heaven so that He can guide their lives to success and fulfilment. Another important action that we as parents should do, is to give our children back to God spiritually. There should be three occasions in a person's life when God must be honoured as the Father. The first and second time starts with the parents when they dedicate their child to God. Firstly, when the child is conceived and is starting to grow in the mother's womb. Through this obedience, we give our child the best protection against the enemy of this world right from the start. Secondly, when the child is born and the parents publicly dedicate their child to God. Luke 2:22 confirms Jesus' dedication publicly "When the time came for the purification rites required by the Law of Moses, Joseph and Mary took Jesus to Jerusalem to present Him to the Lord." Churches have different ceremonies and some call it a dedication service, others call it infant baptism. Parents dedicate their child to God and ask for grace and wisdom in carrying out their responsibilities in bringing up the child. They also pray that their child might one day trust Jesus Christ as their Saviour and for the forgiveness of their sins. Of course, every parent will look after and protect his or her child to the best of their ability, but no parent can give a child the protection and guidance that Almighty God can. He sees and hears everything at all times.

The third very important occasion is when your child gives his or her life to the Lord themselves. This time in their life is when they understand what it means to be a follower of Jesus Christ. They repent of their sins and agree to live for Him who bought them with His precious blood on the cross. This is such a joyous time in heaven amongst the Angels. Luke 15:10 reads "In the same way, I tell you, there is rejoicing in the presence of the angels of God over one sinner who repents." Usually, this public confession occurs through water baptism, where the child or adult is immersed underwater in a bath, pool, river, dam, or sea. Water baptism symbolises the move from death to life. The entrance into the water identifies us with Christ's death on the cross, His burial in the tomb, and His resurrection from the dead. Coming up from the water signifies the brand new life in Christ. We bury the 'old life' and rise to walk in a 'new life'. Baptism also symbolises that the person loves, trusts, and puts their hope in Christ. Even Jesus himself was baptised, in identification with us. Luke 3:23 states that Jesus was about thirty years old when he started His public ministry on earth that lasted around three years.

During this time He was baptised by His cousin, John the Baptist. Jesus was around thirty-three years old when He died on the cross.

Colossians 2:12-14 describes the baptism as follows: "Having been buried with Him in baptism, in which you were also raised with Him through your faith in the working of God, who raised Him from the dead. When you were dead in your sins and in the uncircumcision of your flesh, God made you alive with Christ. He forgave us all our sins, having cancelled the charge of our legal indebtedness, which stood against us and condemned us; He has taken it away, nailing it to the cross." Even Romans 6:4 says "We were therefore buried with Him through baptism into death in order that, just as Christ was raised from the dead through the glory of the Father, we too may live a new life."

We can be water baptised at any age. I have heard of children from the age of six to adults in their late eighties or early nineties being baptised. The general rule is that we must understand what baptism symbolises, and why we want to do it. My own daughter was seven years old when she was present at her grandad's baptism ceremony. She also wanted to be baptised with her grandad. She was almost to the point of desperation. Knowing that some Churches expect you to attend a few classes or meetings with the preacher so that he can make sure you are doing it for the right reasons, I knew she would not be allowed to be baptised on the spot. She was in tears, and I had great difficulty in calming her down and stopping her from jumping in the baptism pool with her grandad. I told her she needed to understand what baptism means before she could be baptised. She insisted that she knew. So I promised her that when we got home, I would baptise her in the bath. As we were driving home that day, I asked her what it means to her to be baptised. I cannot exactly remember her answer, but I do remember that I was amazed at her understanding, and realised that she knew exactly what it was all about. This happened during the year 2001, and as I had promised, that afternoon there was a baptism in our home bath with not only her but also her younger sister. You see, as all of this was unfolding, my younger daughter was listening to our conversations all the way, from the time we watched Grandad being baptised, to when we got home a few hours later. When I got everything ready for our home baptism, she also wanted me to baptise her. We had a session beforehand where I explained baptism to them, then asked them why they wanted to be baptised. When I was satisfied with their responses, we performed the baptism.

In my heart, I felt this was only to calm them down, and as a mother, I thought they were still classified as children, who belong to God anyway. They always remember their bath baptism. As their church friends were baptised in their late teens and asked them if they were baptised, they believed that they were already. For them the bath baptism meant something. In the end, both of them made a commitment again around their early twenties and were baptised in a river through their Church, with a group of people. I am only telling you this story to make you realise that as parents we must never underestimate the mind and understanding of a young child. If I had the time over with the understanding I have today, I would definitely give them the chance to be baptised through a proper water baptism ceremony, as it would have been so much more special to them.

All the people on this earth belong to Jesus, no matter what nationality, gender, or age. Galatians 3:28 states this clearly "There is neither Jew nor Gentile, neither slave nor free, nor is there male and female, for you are all one in Christ Jesus." Let's celebrate who God has made each of us to be. God is no respecter of persons! Peter confirms this in Acts 10:34-35 "I now realise how true it is that God does not show favouritism, but accepts from every nation the one who fears Him and does what is right." Today there are amazing prophets, preachers, and children of God that come from all walks of life and nationalities. Be as Jesus, and accept your brother and sister in Christ no matter who they are or where they grew up.

Take up Your Crown

Never doubt that you are royalty in Christ Jesus! The crucifixion of Jesus instantly made us sons and daughters of God the Father. Jesus is our elder Brother, who is the head of us all. He was awarded Sonship with God the Father. Although we do not fully understand the Trinity (God the Father, God the Son, and God the Holy Spirit) now, we will understand one day in heaven when God will reveal this mystery to us. 1 Corinthians 13:9-10 says "For we know in part and we prophesy in part, but when completeness comes, what is in part disappears."

In 1 Peter 2:9-10 we read "But you are a chosen people, a royal priesthood, a holy nation, God's special possession, that you may declare the praises of Him who called you out of darkness into His wonderful light. Once you were not a people, but now you are the people of God; once you had not received mercy, but now you have received mercy." The time referred to in this scripture where we were not His people, was straight after the fall of man in the Garden of Eden, until the death and resurrection of Jesus.

In his second letter to Timothy, the Apostle Paul wrote in 2 Timothy 4:8, "Now there is in store for me the crown of righteousness, which the Lord, the righteous Judge, will award to me on that day – and not only to me but also to all who have longed for his appearing." Isaiah 62:3 reads "You will be a crown of splendour in the Lord's hand, a royal diadem in the hand of your God." 1 Peter 5:4 says when the Chief Shepherd appears, you will receive the crown of glory that will never fade away. The Chief Shepherd refers to Jesus in His second coming. Mark 13:33 advises us to be on guard and to be alert for Jesus' second coming. God is so faithful that He gave us signs in the Bible of specific events that will happen on earth when the time is coming closer. This way His children can ensure they are ready so they will inherit eternal life. Read Luke 21:5-28 about the warning signs. As children of God, we can walk around with our Spiritual crowns already here on earth, without being arrogant, but confident that we belong to the Father and King of all creation.

If you are not sure whether your parents dedicated you to God when you were born, you have the opportunity now to dedicate yourself, your children, and everything you own to God in order to receive the blessings He wants to give to you.

Lift up your hands to God while you pray the following prayer out loud:

God our Father, Jesus Christ my Lord; forgive me for when I have tried to run my life on my own without recognizing that I belong to You.

Jesus, thank you for giving your life for me, and that You bought me at a price.

Today I am giving my life back to You. I am dedicating myself, my children, my finances and everything I own to you Lord, who is the rightful owner.

Holy Spirit help me to get rid of all the hindrances in my life so that I can hear your voice more clearly every day. Guide me on the way forward to avoid harm. Teach me God's wonderful words and Bible wisdom.

Almighty God, please release the full blessings you have planned for my life.

Wherever life takes me, I know You are in control.

I bless you God our Father, Jesus Christ our Saviour, and Holy Spirit our Helper.

In Jesus' Name.

Amen and Amen!

ELLEN JOUBERT

God's Love Letter to You

Dear Child,

Before I formed you in the womb I knew you. (Jeremiah 1:5 ESV)

You are fearfully and wonderfully made. (Psalm 139:14 NIV)

I knitted you together in your mother's womb. (Psalm 139:13 NIV)

When you pass through the waters, I will be with you; and through the rivers, they shall not overwhelm you; when you walk through fire you shall not be burned, and the flame shall not consume you. (Isaiah 43:2 ESV)

Fear not, for I am with you; be not dismayed, for I am your God; I will strengthen you, I will help you, I will uphold you with my righteous right hand. (Isaiah 41:10 ESV)

Nothing will be able to separate you from the love of God in Christ Jesus our Lord. (Romans 8:39 ESV)

For I, the Lord your God, hold your right hand; it is I who say to you, "Fear not, I am the one who helps you." (Isaiah 41:13 ESV)

My love has been poured into your heart through the Holy Spirit who has been given to you. (Romans 5:5 ESV)

There is no fear in love, but perfect love casts out fear. For fear has to do with punishment, and whoever fears has not been perfected in love. (1 John 4:18 ESV)

For I am the perfect Father. (Matthew 5:48 ESV)

Every good gift that you receive comes from Me. (James 1:17 ESV)

If you seek Me with all your heart, you will find Me. (Deuteronomy 4:29 ESV)

I am your Heavenly Father, and I love you as I love my son, Jesus. (John 17:23 ESV)

I am the Lord that is merciful and gracious, slow to anger and abounding in steadfast love. (Psalm 103:8 ESV)

If you accept the gift of my son Jesus, you accept Me. (1 John 2:23 NIV)

And nothing will ever separate you from My love again. (Romans 8:38-39 NIV)

With love, your Father in Heaven.

CHAPTER 4

Our Countenance and Appearance are Important to the Lord

Parents like to brag about their children because they are part of their flesh and usually look a bit like both parents, or maybe more like one. Personality-wise, kids also inherit some of the characteristics of their parents. As parents, we want the best for our children. Some parents even dress their children so beautifully because they want to show them off to the world as if to say 'Hi, look at my beautiful child! He or she is mine. I created him/her and I love him/her!' Well, that is how God our Father feels about you!

I believe that children of God on this earth need to stand out in appearance, in the love that they show towards others, in wisdom, and in character. They must be confident, but not arrogant. Confidence is made up of what we are feeling, what we are thinking, what we know, and what our opinion is of ourselves. Accepting who God has created us to be and not wanting to be like someone else, but working towards the best version of ourselves that we can be, overcoming our failures and trying again. Confidence in oneself is very necessary to succeed in all of life's challenges. When confidence steps in, fear steps out. The fear of failing and of what others think of us will disappear. However, we cannot hurt, trick, and steal and then not worry what others think of us. Always try to live your life with a good character. This includes all the aspects of a person's behaviour and attitude that make up his or her personality. The qualities of a good character are described in scriptures throughout the Bible. They are to love God, to be honest in all your dealings, to always be a person of integrity, to have a generous spirit, treating others with respect, loving others as you love yourself, having an attitude of gratitude, being trustworthy, not looking only for self-gain, being self-disciplined, having self-control, not being self-absorbed, being fair in everything and to everyone, not stealing, not murdering, not hurting someone intentionally, not being afraid to fail, not having an attitude that the world owes you something and that you do not have to do your part, and having compassion for others.

Over the years of coaching children, young adults, and women, I noticed that as they grew in confidence it showed in their eyes, and their faces would light up. The eyes of a child or adult who lacks confidence will reflect it. The best way of describing it for those of you who have or had a pet dog is that when your dog has done something wrong it cannot look you in the eyes. Their ears lie flat against their head, and even their tail will be droopy. That is how a person appears in the world when they do not have confidence. In the spirit world that is how the devil wants to see God's children, defeated, and with no confidence. Satan knows he does not stand a chance to mess with people who see themselves as Kingdom children and who have confidence in God, Jesus Christ, and the Holy Spirit.

When I say that God wants us to have a good and healthy countenance, the word 'countenance' refers to our face, including facial features, expressions, and appearance. A person doesn't have to have the most attractive facial features to be beautiful. That is what my book *How to Look and Feel Younger for Longer* is all about. It gives advice on how an individual can improve their appearance through simple everyday practices. There is no ugly child or adult on this earth. God has made us all wonderfully! That is what He says in the Bible. That means we are all made beautiful. Not one person on this earth looks the same though, except for identical twins or someone referred to as another person's double, but there will still be differences in their appearance. God has created us all uniquely. There are different kinds of beauty in this world and that is why people do not look the same. How boring or even confusing would it be if, for example, you had five children and they all looked the same?

Are there people who can improve their countenance and appearance? Yes of course! Some people mismanage their weight, others mismanage their health through unhealthy eating habits, and not enough movement or exercise, some compromise hygienic standards running the risk of falling ill, and others may mismanage their personal growth by not building their knowledge and brain. Because of a lack of knowledge in these areas, many people may not look after their body as wisely as God expects us to. The Bible says we have to glorify God in everything we do (1 Corinthians 10:31), including preserving our bodies for Him as long as we can. Does that mean we have to get a face lift, cosmetic surgery, anti-wrinkle injections, or fillers to preserve our youth-look forever? No! He just wants us to show respect to our body and age gracefully. Is it a sin to make use of these external services to help you look beautiful for longer? No! But it does become a sin if you are obsessed with the appearance of your face and body, to the point where you start changing who God created you to be.

Another question to ask is: For whom are you making these extreme changes to your body? If the focus is to impress others, rather than pleasing God, it becomes a sin. When you spend more money on your outside appearance than you would spend to advance the Kingdom of God, your focus is also wrong, and you are starting to idolize your body. An idol is anything that gets between us and God, and it is whatever we treasure more than God. God wants His children to have a good countenance and appearance, but He does not want us to let our body become an idol.

In 1 Corinthians 6:19-20 we read why it is important to the Lord that we look after our bodies "Do you not know that your bodies are temples of the Holy Spirit, who is in you, whom you have received from God? You are not your own; you were bought at a price. Therefore honour God with your bodies." Our body today is described by God as the temple of the Holy Spirit and therefore it is a command that we must look after our body both inside and outside. From the inside through healthy eating habits and exercise, and from the outside in how we appear. In the Old Testament, God gave specific instructions to Moses in Exodus 26 for how the Tabernacle should look like, and in 1 King 6, King Solomon built the temple according to God's instructions.

In 1 Chronicles 28, King David told fellow Israelites that in his heart he wanted to build a house as a place of rest for the Ark of the Covenant of the Lord, for the footstool of our God, and he made plans to build it, but God said to him in verse 3 that he is not to build a house for His Name, because he is a warrior and has shed blood. Then God said in verse 6 "Solomon your son is the one who will build My house and My courts, for I have chosen him to be My son, and I will be his father." In 1 Chronicles 28:11-12 David gave Solomon all the plans for the temple, its buildings, its storerooms, its upper parts, its inner rooms, and the place of atonement, as the Holy Spirit instructed him to build it. When you read through the Bible books Exodus 26 and 1 King 6, you'll notice how specific God was on the structure and interior design. I am sure you will agree with me that God is a person of taste and style. That is why God wants us to be people of taste and style today, by looking after our bodily temple that houses His Holy Spirit.

Jesus Christ's Magnificent Appearance At His Second Coming

The 'Second Coming' is referring to when Jesus Christ will return to earth in fulfilment of His promises and the prophecies made about Him in the Bible. Jesus will come back at a time when the world is most in need of a righteous King. He was despised and rejected at His 'First Coming' over two thousand years ago because He came in humility and love to fulfil the crucifixion and resurrection. His 'Second Coming' will be very different! It will be the greatest demonstration ever of His Lordship over all. He is coming to wage war against all that is evil. This time there will be no doubt to all people, those who have already died, and those who are still living, that He is the King of kings and Lord of lords. The book of Revelation, chapters 6-18, describe the times prior to the 'Second Coming' of Jesus, to help his people recognize when the time is near.

In Revelation 16:15 Jesus says "Look, I come like a thief! Blessed is the one who stays awake and remains clothed, so as not to go naked and be shamefully exposed." Clothed in terms of:

- Accepting Jesus Christ.
- Loving God the Father with all your heart.
- Not grieving the Holy Spirit.
- Showing God's love for others.
- Being a person of good character.
- Being clothed with the righteousness of Christ.
- Regularly studying the Bible.
- Being watchful for end time signs.

Being watchful does not mean looking at the sky for signs all the time, but being clothed with all these good characteristics and being ready at any time for when Jesus comes back.

We must also prepare the world for His return, by discipling people, thus making the earth a place where God's commands are obeyed, and where more of His love is displayed. Ephesians 4:26 says "In your anger do not sin. Do not let the sun go down while you are still angry." It is the will of Christ that we forgive and be reconciled. The night that we may be in rebellion against His will, may be the night that He comes like a thief, and we will be caught naked and not clothed. We must be properly clothed at all times by living in obedience to the will of God. In 1 Thessalonians 5:2-5 Paul wrote to the church of the Thessalonians warning them "For you yourselves know perfectly that the day of the Lord so comes as a thief in the night. For when they say, peace and safety, then sudden destruction comes upon them, as labour pains upon a pregnant woman. And they shall not escape. But you, brethren, are not in darkness, so that this Day should overtake you as a thief. You are all sons of light and sons of the day. We are not of the night nor of darkness." When He was on earth during His first coming, Jesus said in Matthew 24:36 that the day and hour of His 'Second Coming' is not known to Him, and that only God the Father knows when that will be.

Revelation 19:7-8 says "Let us be glad and rejoice and give Him glory, for the marriage of the Lamb (Jesus) has come, and His wife (the Church) has made herself ready. And to her, it was granted to be arrayed in fine linen, clean and bright, for the fine linen is the righteous acts of the saints". The main concern is not when the 'Second Coming' of Jesus is going to be, but are we going to be clothed for it?

Revelation 19:11-16 describes how Jesus will be clothed at His 'Second Coming'. He will be sitting on a white horse and will be called *Faithful* and *True*. His eyes will be blazing fire and on His head will be many crowns. There will be a name written on Him that no one knows but He Himself. He will be clothed in a red coloured robe and His name is the 'Word of God'. The armies of heaven will be following Him riding on white horses, and they will be clothed in fine linen that is white and clean.

The colour red is often associated with war because it is the shade of blood. When Christ returns, it is as a Man of War, meeting the long-awaited judgment. On His thigh, He will have the name written:

KING OF KINGS AND LORD OF LORDS.

CHAPTER 5

Do Everything as if You are Doing it For the Lord

> "And whatever you do, do it heartily, as to the Lord and not to men, knowing that from the Lord you will receive the reward of the inheritance; for you serve the Lord Christ" - Colossians 3:23-24

We respect God and His gift of the Holy Spirit within us, by respecting and caring for our body. 'Do everything as if you are doing it for the Lord' may sound controlling, but God is LOVE and all He really wants is love and respect in return. We love God because He first loves us in that while we were yet sinners, Christ died for us (Romans 5:8). That is why He has given us a free will because forced love is not love at all. He does not want to force us to love Him. God wants us to see how good He is to us, and that we will love Him because He is so good. God's love is very different from how He teaches us to love others. His love towards us is unconditional and we do not have to please Him first before He loves us. He loves us no matter what. He is LOVE and there is nothing that we can do that will make Him love us more than He already does. It does not matter what bad things we have done or where we have been in life, He loves us! That is the full meaning of unconditional love.

1 John 4:7-21 explains God's loving nature "Dear friends, let us love one another, for love comes from God. Everyone who loves has been born of God and knows God. Whoever does not love does not know God, because God is love. This is how God showed His love among us: He sent His one and only Son into the world that we might live through Him. This is love: not that we loved God, but that He loved us and sent His Son as an atoning sacrifice for our sins. Dear friends, since God so loved us, we also ought to love one another. No one has ever seen God; but if we love one another, God lives in us and His love is made complete in us. This is how we know that we live in Him and He in us: He has given us of His Spirit, and we have seen and testify that the Father has sent His Son to be the Saviour of the world. If anyone acknowledges that Jesus is the Son of God, God lives in them and they in God. And so we know and rely on the love God has for us. God is love. Whoever lives in love lives in God, and God in them. This is how love is made complete among us so that we will have confidence on the day of judgment: In this world, we are like Jesus. There is no fear in love. But perfect love drives out fear because fear has to do with punishment. The one who fears is not made perfect in love. We love because He first loved us. Whoever claims to love God yet hates a brother or sister is a liar. For whoever does not love their brother and sister, whom they have seen, cannot love God, whom they have not seen. And He has given us this command: Anyone who loves God must also love their brother and sister."

As you have read through this book, you have seen that God has done everything and is still doing everything for His children because of His deep love for us. Frankly, I cannot understand why anyone would not want to love and serve such a good and loving God.

When one of the experts in the law asked Jesus in Matthew 22:36, "Teacher, which is the greatest commandment in the Law?" Jesus replied in Matthew 22:37-38 "Love the Lord your God with all your heart and with all your soul and with all your mind. This is the first and greatest commandment". Some people view this commandment to love God, as a commandment of feelings which they have no control over. The love that God wants us to have for Him is not based on a feeling and is more of an attitude and an act. A person can influence their feelings, by controlling their thoughts and actions. Loving God means believing in Him, trusting Him, and obeying Him. 1 John 5:1-3 describes how we must love God "Everyone who believes that Jesus is the Christ is born of God, and everyone who loves the father loves his child as well. This is how we know that we love the children of God: by loving God and carrying out His commands. In fact, this is love for God: to keep His commands. And His commands are not burdensome."

A full description of how we must love our brothers and sisters here on earth is explained in 1 Corinthians 13:4-7:

4. "Love is patient, love is kind. It does not envy, it does not boast, it is not proud.

5. It does not dishonour others, it is not self-seeking, it is not easily angered, it keeps no record of wrongs.

6. Love does not delight in evil but rejoices with the truth.

7. It always protects, trusts, hopes, and perseveres".

The Four Types of Love Described in the Bible

The four unique forms of love that we find in the Bible are communicated through four Greek words: Eros, Storge, Philia, and Agape.

- *Eros* (Pronounced: AIR-ohs) is sensual or romantic love. The Bible limits erotic or sexual love to married couples. Although this Greek term 'eros' does not appear in the Bible, it is portrayed in the Old Testament in the 'Song of Songs'. In 1 Corinthians 7:8-9 Apostle Paul also says "Now to the unmarried and the widows I say: It is good for them to stay unmarried, as I do. But if they cannot control themselves, they should marry, for it is better to marry than to burn with passion". Lust is an unlawful desire; therefore it is better to get married rather than desiring to be with someone, or to go outside God's Word by being with someone outside of marriage. Eros love was made by God and it is beautiful, but it is for one man and one woman joined together for life.

- *Storge* (Pronounced: STOR-jay) describes family love and is the affectionate bond that develops naturally between parents and children, and brothers and sisters. Romans 12:10 says this "Love one another with brotherly affection. Outdo one another in showing honour."

- *Philia* (Pronounced: FILL-ee-uh) is the most general type of love in Scripture, encompassing love for fellow humans, care, respect, and compassion for people in need. Jesus said philia would identify his followers "By this everyone will know that you are my disciples if you love one another" – John 13:35. Jesus also told us that we must love our enemies "But I say to you, love your enemies and pray for those who persecute you" – Matthew 5:44. This is Philia love!

- *Agape* (Pronounced: Uh-GAH-pay) is the highest form of love in the Bible. This term defines God's immeasurable, incomparable love for humankind. This divine love that comes from God is perfect, unconditional, sacrificial, and pure. The Bible is full of scriptures describing God's perfect 'Agape love' towards us and John 15:13 says it beautifully "Greater love has no one than this, that one lay down his life for his friends." Agape love caused Jesus to sacrifice His life for us.

Jesus' Second Coming

The Bible is the 'manual of life' that God provided for us. In 2 Timothy 3:16-17 it says "All Scripture is God-breathed and is useful for teaching, rebuking, correcting and training in righteousness, so that the servant of God may be thoroughly equipped for every good work." When you buy any new electrical appliance you'll always receive an instruction manual with it, teaching you how to best care for it. When the care instructions are followed it will operate at its best and last for much longer. Therefore keep reading the Bible to understand who God is, what He has done for us, and how to live a long and prosperous life.

Important subjects that the Bible teaches us:

- How much Father God, Jesus, and the Holy Spirit loves us.
- That we do not belong to ourselves, but to a loving God.
- How to protect ourselves from evil.
- How to recognize evil coming into our life.
- The signs to watch for when Jesus' 'Second Coming' is near.

These signs will help us to make sure our life is ready when Jesus returns to gather all the children of God on this earth. All people who had already died, and those still living, who accepted Jesus Christ at the time of His return, will be living with the Trinity, and their saved brothers and sisters in Christ for all eternity.

Although no one knows exactly when Jesus will return to earth, we know that at that time there will be a lot of misery and pain. It will be the darkest point in the earth's history when evil and unrighteousness will rule the world. The Bible talks about a tribulation period on the earth which will last for seven years. Refer to the following scriptures: Daniel 9:27, Daniel 12:1-3, Matthew 24:15-22, Revelation 11:2 and Revelation 13:5. Some teachers, teaching on the end time prophecies believe the saints will be removed before the great tribulation, and others believe we'll be taken away halfway through the seven years of tribulation. All Christians do not agree on every detail of what will occur in the final events of this world's history. Some of these events and their order of occurrence have simply not been made clear in the Bible. Either way, I think we have to be aware of this time, and Jesus will reveal everything closer to the time.

1 Thessalonians 4:16-17 says this, when Jesus will return "For the Lord himself will descend from heaven with a cry of command, with the voice of an archangel, and with the sound of the trumpet of God. The dead who were born again during their lifetime will be resurrected first and caught up together in the clouds to meet the Lord Jesus in the air. Those who are still alive will be immediately after that also be lifted up in the air to meet Jesus. This is known as the Rapture. And so we will be with the Lord forever (Matthew 24:30, 2 Thessalonians 1:7, Revelation 1:7). This removal of the multitudes of saved people will be evident on the earth. There will be no doubt anymore and everyone will know that Jesus is the Lord and Saviour of this world. This period is where everyone left on earth will experience worldwide hardships, disasters, famine, war, pain, and suffering, which will wipe out more than seventy-five per cent of all life on the earth before the 'Second Coming' of Jesus takes place.

At the end of this current earth, is when the Anti-Christ and his worldly armies will move on to Jerusalem to wage war against God's people, the Jews. This is the time when Jesus will come back and descend from the Mount of Olives in Jerusalem to fight against those nations who oppose His leadership. This is one of the last signs, according to the Bible, when Jesus will return for good. Jesus, the angel armies, and His saints (those Christians who are born again and sanctified as holy) who were raptured before will return to earth with Him to defeat all His enemies (Zechariah 14:1-4). He will also destroy those who destroyed the earth according to Revelation 11:18.

The Anti-Christ and False Prophet are the first ones to be thrown into the Lake of Fire and Brimstone. Satan will be bound in the bottomless pit for a thousand years. At the start of these thousand years, Jesus will take over all the kingdoms on earth to rule it in peace. He will appoint His saints to help rule over the nations under His authority (Revelation 5:10).

When Jesus' thousand years of reign is finished, Satan will be released for a short time, and he will deceive people for the last time. Revelation 20:7-10 describes the judgment of Satan "When the thousand years are over, Satan will be released from his prison and will go out to deceive the nations in the four corners of the earth - Gog and Magog - and to gather them for battle. In number, they are like the sand on the seashore. They marched across the breadth of the earth and surrounded the camp of God's people, the City He loves. But fire came down from heaven and devoured them. And the devil, who deceived them, was thrown into the lake of burning sulfur, where the beast and the false prophet had been thrown. They will be tormented day and night forever and ever".

At the end of the thousand years' reign, all those who have rejected Jesus Christ will come before the *Great White Throne of Judgment*. They will then also be cast into the Lake of Fire. In Revelation 20:12-13 we learn about the people at this Judgment, "I saw the dead, small and great, standing before God…The sea gave up the dead who were in it, and Death and Hades delivered up the dead who were in them."

Now that Satan, all of his fallen angels, all God's enemies, and unsaved humanity have been cast into the Lake of Fire and Brimstone, God will now be giving the rest of saved humanity their final reward – the New Heaven and New Earth.

This does not mean the earth will be destroyed or disappear totally, as many believe. Why would God say in the beginning after He created the earth that everything was good, and then wants to destroy it? I believe that He will destroy everything that is evil and became part of His good creation. The earth will be renewed or maybe another way to look at it, improved. Let's look at the following scriptures that describe the new heaven and earth.

Revelation 21:1-5

"Now I saw a new heaven and a new earth, for the first heaven and the first earth had passed away. Also, there was no more sea. Then I, John, saw the holy city, **New Jerusalem, coming down out of heaven from God**, prepared as a bride adorned for her husband. And I heard a loud voice from heaven saying, **Behold, the tabernacle of God is with men, and He will dwell with them**, and they shall be His people. **God Himself will be with them and be their God**. And God will wipe away every tear from their eyes; there shall be no more death, nor sorrow, nor crying. There shall be no more pain, for the former things have passed away. Then He who sat on the throne said, **"Behold, I make all things new"**. And He said to me, "Write, for these words are true and faithful."

From the above passage, John who was shown all the end-time prophecies by Jesus, tells us in verse 1 that the new earth will have no more sea. Jesus will rule the earth from Jerusalem. It also says that God the Father will make His dwelling place among His people.

By reading further in Revelation 21:22-27 it describes the new city, Jerusalem:

"But I saw **no temple** in it, for the Lord God Almighty and the Lamb (Jesus) are its temple. The **city had no need of the sun or of the moon to shine in it**, for the glory of God illuminated it. The Lamb (Jesus) is its light. And the nations of those who are saved shall walk in its light, and the kings of the earth bring their glory and honour into it. **Its gates shall not be shut at all by day** (there shall be no night there). And they shall bring the glory and the honour of the nations into it. But **there shall by no means enter it anything that defiles**, or causes an abomination or a lie, but **only those who are written in the Lamb's Book of Life**".

What a wonderful time to look forward to! My prayer is that you will be clothed and ready for Jesus Christ's return.

Until we are properly clothed for the King,
we cannot walk in extreme victory!

Walking with God every day,
and having a relationship with Him,
will secure our eternal life with Him.

ELLEN JOUBERT

My Prayer for You

Dear God,

I pray that You will make yourself known to every reader of this book.

Give them a heart and desire to know You as the Trinity (Father, Son, and Holy Spirit), who want to make Your dwelling place inside of their body, as well as their physical house, which they live in here on earth.

Give them Your peace and rest so that they will trust You in who You say You are, and what You want to do for them, on earth and in heaven.

Bless them with the best gifts that you have planned for their life.

Give them the heart to know that every good gift comes from You and belongs to You.

Protect them from the devil and his demons and rebuke the devourer from their life for your Name's sake, as you promise in Malachi 3:11.

I declare that poverty and hardship are broken by the power of the Holy Spirit over their lives and their children's lives.

I break the hold of every sickness that they may have in the Name of Jesus Christ. Their body is healthy and rejuvenated in Jesus' wonderful name. Lord, teach them how to eat and live a healthy life to preserve their body for You. Give them the knowledge and determination to stay on the healthy living path that You will guide them on.

Let them walk in a supernatural breakthrough every day.

Lord bless them and keep them. Make Your face shine on them and be gracious to them. Lord turn Your face toward them and give them peace.

I pray this in Jesus Christ's Name.

Amen and Amen.

Your Five-Week Study Guide

WEEK 1 – Clothed for the King

1. Jesus Christ our Lord and Saviour is the King of all kings and the Lord of all lords that was, is, and is to come on this earth. Following are two Bible verses to confirm it.
   (Write down the scriptures from your Bible or refer to page 23)

   Revelation 17:14

   _____

   _____

   _____

   _____

   _____

   Revelation 19:16

   _____

   _____

   _____

   _____

   _____

2. Genesis 1 describes that God created the earth and everything in it in six days. Complete the following on what God created on which day. (refer to pages 24-25)

Day 1 - _____

Day 2 - _____

Day 3 - _____

Day 4 - _____

Day 5 - _____

Day 6 - _____

Day 7 - "Thus the heavens and the earth were completed in all their vast array. By the seventh day, God had finished the work He had been doing; so on the seventh day, He rested from all His work. Then God blessed this day and made it holy because on it he rested from all the work of creating that He had done" – Genesis 2:1-3.

Day Seven, therefore, was made holy and God commanded us to rest after six days of work. God has done this for a reason because our body needs rest to recharge for the following six days of work. This 'Holy Day' is declared by God so that we can plug into the Spiritual realm through worshipping Him and studying His Word daily so that we can stay connected to Him. In Proverbs 4:20-22 God says "My son, pay attention to what I say; turn your ear to my words. Do not let them out of your sight, keep them within your heart; for they are life to those who find them and health to one's whole body".

Through staying connected to God He teaches us in His Word, that He will reveal to us present and future things through the Holy Spirit who will guide us into our 'promised land'.

> Your *Promised Land* means the geographic area or territory which God wants to plant you in where you will be blessed on all levels of your life. A land that is flowing with milk and honey (Ezekiel 20:6). This means you will have no shortage in your life and will live a good life.

3. In Genesis 1:26 God said "Let US make mankind in OUR _____, in OUR _____, so that they may rule over the fish in the sea and the birds in the sky, over the livestock and all the wild animals, and over all the creatures that move along the ground." (refer to page 25)

What does this scripture mean to you?

_____
_____
_____
_____
_____
_____

4. The devil orchestrated the fall of mankind in the Garden of Eden. Describe how the 'fall of mankind' (Adam and Eve and all future generations) happened in short according to Genesis 3: (refer to page 27)

_____

_____

_____

5. What was the perfect plan of God to reverse the fallen state of mankind forever? (refer to page 29)

_____

_____

_____

6. The ten key components in life on how we have to be clothed for our King are: (refer to pages 31-60)

    1) Clothed with Confidence.
    2) Clothed with Salvation.
    3) Clothed with the Holy Spirit.
    4) Clothed with Righteousness.
    5) Clothed with Health and Happiness.
    6) Clothed with Prosperity.
    7) Clothed with Knowledge and Wisdom.
    8) Clothed with the Armour of God.
    9) Clothed with Style and Beauty.
    10) Clothed with Humility.

CLOTHED FOR THE KING

Name and describe in short what each component means to you:

1. _____

   _____

   _____

   _____

   _____

2. _____

   _____

   _____

   _____

   _____

3. _____

   _____

   _____

   _____

   _____

4.

5.

6.

7.

8.

9.

10.

WEEK 2 - There is NO Greater Love Than This!

> "For God so loved the world, that He gave His only Son (Jesus), that whoever believes in Him should not perish but have eternal life" - John 3:16

1. What does John 3:16 mean to you? (refer to page 63)

   _____

   _____

   _____

   _____

   _____

2. Complete the following: (refer to page 64)

   The devil was one of the chief angels made by God in heaven and his name was Lucifer at that time, meaning

   _____ or

   _____.

Lucifer was established by God to be the angel of worship, one whose ministry surrounded the heart of heaven. According to Ezekiel 28:13 Lucifer had been placed in Eden, that is the garden of God. He could freely move around in heaven and dwell in the presence of God continually. To dwell in the presence of a perfect God, Lucifer had to be perfect. From the day he was created he was blameless in his ways until wickedness was found in him.

What was this wickedness according to Ezekiel 28:17? (refer to pages 64-65)

_____

_____

_____

3. When Lucifer was banished from living in heaven his name changed from Lucifer to Satan meaning (refer to page 64)

_____.

4. Why does the devil want to keep corrupting God's children? (refer to pages 64-66)

_____

_____

_____

_____

_____

_____

_____

_____

5. After Lucifer was stripped of his name and glory of 'Morning Star' it was given to a far more deserving individual, the Son of God. Revelation 22:16 confirms that Jesus is now named the bright *Morning Star*. (Write down this scripture from your Bible or refer to page 66)

Revelation 22:16 -

_____

_____

_____

6. According to Psalm 1:1-2 there are three things we must NOT DO and two things we MUST DO to be blessed. (refer to page 67)

    - The three things not to do are: Not walk in the counsel of the ungodly; Not stand in the path of sinners; and not sit in the seat of the scornful.
    - The two things we must do: Delight in the law of the Lord, and meditate on His laws day and night.

When you follow these do's and don'ts how will you be blessed according to Psalm 1:3? (refer to your Bible or page 67)

_____

_____

_____

_____

WEEK 3 – We Belong to the King!

1. A message that we often hear is that Jesus's crucifixion paid the price for our salvation and restored our relationship with God the Father, which instantly made us sons and daughters of God the Father. The other very important message is that the cross of Jesus bought us and we now belong to Him, and He belongs to God the Father.

> 1 Corinthians 6:19 says "Or do you not know that your body is the temple of the Holy Spirit who is in you, whom you have from God, and you are not your own? For you were bought at a price; therefore glorify God in your body and in your spirit, which are God's."

The cross of Jesus restored our relationship with God the Father to the original relationship that Adam and Eve enjoyed with Him, but with an added benefit.

What is this benefit? (refer to page 70)

_____
_____
_____
_____

2. The devil still has many tricks up his sleeve today to corrupt God's children and get a foot in the door to start working in their lives. What are some of the obvious ones to recognize when the devil is working in someone's life? (refer to page 70)

_____

_____

_____

_____

_____

_____

3. If it was not for Jesus who came to earth and died for us, we would all perish. Because of the Cross, we can live forever, but only if we decide to accept God's gift to us. Accepting this free gift and giving your life to the Lord gives you nine privileges. What are these nine privileges? (refer to pages 71-75)

1. _____

2. _____

3. _____

4. _____

5. _____

6. _____

7. _____

8. _____

9. _____

4. Every child and adult wants to feel they belong to a family. That is how we were created. God created us as His family, which belongs together. This is why children and adults desire to belong to a family all the time. When a child is born he or she belongs to God first, before they belong to their earthly parents because it is God who forms every child in the mother's womb according to the Bible. No matter what, your first parent figure in life should be God the Father. (refer to page 76)

Psalm 139:13 says "_____

_____

_____

_____"

5. This sense of belonging creates that inner_____

and will produce a happier_____.
(refer to page 76)

6. For the best protection against the enemy of this world (devil) every parent should dedicate their child publicly to God. Even Jesus was publicly dedicated when the time came, according to the Law of Moses. In Luke 2:22 His parents Joseph and Mary took Him to Jerusalem to present Him to the Lord.

Name the two baby dedications necessary in a child's life: (refer to pages 76-77)

1. _____

2. _____

7. When a child grows up there is another occasion when they give their own life to the Lord. This is called *Water Baptism*. This time in their life is when they understand what it means to be a follower of Jesus Christ.

What is the Spiritual meaning of *Water Baptism*?
(refer to pages 77-78)

_____

_____

_____

_____

8. What does it mean to you to take up your crown now while you are still here on earth as the child of Almighty God?
(refer to pages 80-81)

_____

_____

_____

9. The Bible is full of God expressing His love to you. Write your 'love letter' to God in the space below:

WEEK 4 - Our Countenance and Appearance are Important to the Lord

1. Why do you think it is important for God that we take care of our countenance and appearance? (refer to pages 85-88)

_____

_____

_____

_____

_____

_____

_____

_____

2. What do you understand when you hear the term Jesus Christ's 'Second Coming'? (refer to pages 89-91)

_____

_____

_____

_____

3. Are you looking forward to Jesus Christ's 'Second Coming'?

   Yes ☐   No ☐

   Why? _____
   _____
   _____
   _____

4. Revelation 16:15 describes Jesus Christ's 'Second Coming' like a thief in the night. It reads: "Look, I come like a thief! Blessed is the one who stays awake and remains clothed, so as not to go naked and be shamefully exposed".

   How can you stay awake to know when the 'Second Coming' is near? (refer to pages 89-90)

   _____
   _____
   _____
   _____
   _____
   _____

5. According to Matthew 24:36 the day and the time of Jesus Christ's 'Second Coming' are not known by the angels or Jesus, but only _____ knows?
(refer to page 90)

6. The last book in the Bible, Revelation chapters 6-18, describe the end times prior to the 'Second Coming' of Jesus to help God's children recognize when the time is coming near for Him to return to earth. Read these chapters in your Bible and write down a few warning signs as described:

_____
_____
_____
_____
_____
_____
_____
_____
_____
_____
_____
_____

7. How will Jesus be clothed at His 'Second Coming' according to Revelations 19:11-16? (refer to your Bible or pages 90-91)

_____

_____

_____

_____

_____

WEEK 5 - Do Everything as if You are doing it For the Lord

1. Having respect for our body that is housing our spirit and God's indwelling Spirit, shows that we respect God and the gift He gave us.

> Colossians 3:23-24 say "And whatever you do, do it heartily, as to the Lord and not to men, knowing that from the Lord you will receive the reward of the inheritance; for you serve the Lord Christ."

God is LOVE and His love for you is_____.
This means He loves you no matter what. There is nothing that you can do that will make Him love you more than He already does. (refer to pages 93-94)

2. In Matthew 22:36 the experts in the law asked Jesus which is the the greatest commandment in the Law. Write down Jesus answer to them: (refer to your Bible or page 95)

_____
_____
_____
_____
_____

3. Describe how we must love our brothers and sisters here on earth according to 1 Corinthians 13:4-7: (refer to your Bible or page 95)

_____
_____
_____
_____
_____
_____
_____

4. The four unique types of love that we find in the Bible are communicated through four Greek words. Name and explain them: (refer to pages 96-97)

   1) _____
   _____
   _____

   2) _____
   _____
   _____

   3) _____
   _____
   _____

   4) _____
   _____
   _____

5. When Jesus returns to earth, in His 'Second Coming' He will destroy _____
   _____ (Revelation 11:18)

6. What will Jesus do after He descended from the Mount of Olives at His 'Second Coming'? (refer to page 99)

_____

_____

7. When Jesus returns at His 'Second Coming', for how long will He reign the earth before Satan will be released for a short time and then cast into the lake of burning sulfur? (refer to page 99)

_____

8. According to Revelation 21:1-5 and 21:22-27 how will the new heaven and earth look like? (refer to pages 100-101)

_____

_____

_____

_____

_____

_____

_____

_____

9. What did you personally take away from reading 'Clothed for the King'?

INDEX

A

The Holy Spirit gives us the **assurance** that we are saved, page 36.
Acts of the flesh, page 39.
Anti-oxidants in our diet protect cells in our body, page 44.
Live your life with the full **Armour of God** on, page 52.
The **Anti-Christ** and his armies will move up to Jerusalem to wage war, page 99.

B

A healthy **brain** will produce a healthy and happy life, page 41.
The human **brain** consists of sixty per cent fat, page 42.
We **belong to God first**, before we belong to our parents, page 76.
Baby dedication, page 77.
Belt of the truth, page 54.
Breastplate of righteousness, page 54.

C

God **created the earth** and everything in it in six days, pages 24-25.
The man was **created good**, page 25.
Confidence originates from our mind, page 40.
The main purpose of Jesus' **crucifixion**, page 69.
How to **communicate with God**, pages 71-72.
God's children must be **confident and not arrogant**, page 81.

Confidence lights up a person's eyes and face, page 86.
God wants us to have a good and healthy **countenance** for Him, page 86.
Clothed correctly for Jesus 'Second Coming', page 89.

D

Do not forget about your **dreams**, page 18.
Always **dress with style and respect** for God, ourselves and others, page 56.
Through the Holy Spirit we have **direct communication with God** again, page 70.
Dedicate yourself to God, page 81.

E

Beauty is only **evil** when it is used for evil, page 58.
Believing and living for Jesus gives us **eternal life**, pages 60-61.

F

The **fall of mankind**, page 27.
Beware of **false prophets**, page 38.
Overproduction of **free radicals** leads to chronic diseases, page 44.
The name 'Christian' means **followers of Christ**, page 60.
Jesus will make known to us **future revelations**, pages 74-75.
Feet with **shoes of gospel and peace**, page 54.

G

God **gave us a free will**, page 33.
God clothed us with the **'garment of salvation'**, page 34.
Bearing **good fruit**, page 39.
God's Love Letter to you, page 82.
The **greatest commandment in the Law**, page 95.

H

God created for Adam a suitable **helper**, page 26.
Foods most **harmful** to the human body, page 45.
Happiness follows when our brain and body is healthy, page 46.
Jesus came in **humility** the first time but will come back in all His Glory, page 60.
Why Satan **hates** the human race? page 65.
Three **occasions** to honour God in our life, page 76.
Helmet of salvation, page 55.

I

Inspiration for the book title and cover image, pages 9-10.
Mankind was created in God's **image**, page 25.
Our **identity** comes from God, pages 32-33.
Walk in your right and **inheritance of being healthy**, page 73.
Are there people who can **improve their countenance and appearance**? page 87.
The new city will have no sun or moon as God will **illuminate** it, page 101.

J

Jesus Christ lived on earth for thirty-three years before He was crucified, page 29.
Jesus promised to always look after us, page 72.

K

Jesus Christ, the **King of kings** and the Lord of Lords, page 23.

L

God **loves** us all and made us beautiful and worthy, page 19.
Lucifer was a chief angel in heaven, page 64.

The full description of **love** according to the Bible, page 95.
Eros **love** (romantic love), page 96.
Philia **love** (general love for others), page 96.
Storge **love** (family love), page 96.
Agape **love** (God's perfect unconditional love), page 97.
God the Father will come and **live amongst His people** in the new earth, page 100.

M

How Ellen **met her husband**, pages 12-14.
Ellen's husband had a dream to **move to Australia**, page 15.
The **marriage of the Lamb** (Jesus) and His bride (The Church), page 35.
Mankind was created spirit, body, and soul, page 26.

N

There is **no ugly child or adult** on this earth, pages 86-87.
A **New Jerusalem** comes down from heaven, page 100.
The new earth will have **no more sea**, page 100.

O

Oxygen for the brain comes through proper breathing and exercise, page 42.
Oxygen plays a major part in all brain functions, page 44.
Oxidative stress occurs when there are too many free radicals in our body, page 44.
Understanding God's **ownership of everything**, page 47.

P

God's **perfect peace** and rest, page 41.
The prophet Samuel anointed David as king of Judah, page 57.
The do's and don'ts for a **prosperous life**, page 67.

Living for the Lord will give you certain **privileges**, pages 71-75.
The Lord will **protect** us from the evil one, page 73.
We must also **prepare the world** for Jesus' return, page 90.
Praying in the Spirit, page 55.

Q

Qualities of a good character described in the Bible, page 86.

R

Jesus was **raised from the dead** by the Holy Spirit, page 29.
Revelation came from the Holy Spirit that Ellen would write books, page 15.
Righteousness is closely related to our character, page 38.
Recognize Satan infiltrating your life, page 70.
We are **royalty in Christ Jesus**, page 80.
We show **respect** to God when we are caring for our body, page 93.
At the end, the earth will be **renewed** by God, page 100.

S

The **serpent** deceived Eve, pages 27-28.
The **Sinners Prayer** to accept Jesus, page 37.
The Prayer of **Salvation**, page 37.
Our **spiritual protection** comes from God, page 52.
Things you can do to **secure God's divine protection**, pages 52-53.
The blood Jesus shed on the cross paid for our **salvation**, page 69.
We are God's **stewards** over all His creation, pages 75-76.
The '**Second Coming**' of Jesus Christ, page 89.
Jesus will be **sitting on a white horse** when He returns, pages 90-91.
Signs to watch for when Jesus' 'Second Coming' is near, page 97.
Shield of faith, page 55.
Sword of the Spirit, page 55.

T

The **ten key components** to be 'Clothed for the King', pages 31-32.
The **Trinity (God, Jesus, Holy Spirit)** worked together in creating mankind, page 32.
The **thief** (Satan) comes to steal, kill, and destroy, page 40.
Every word God gave us in the Bible can be **trusted**, pages 48-49.
Jesus will come back like a **thief in the night**, page 89.
The start of Jesus' **thousand-year reign**, page 99.

U

The full meaning of **unconditional love**, pages 93-94.

V

Extreme **Victory** comes from being properly clothed for the King, page 101.

W

Some churches are **weak**, page 39.
Wisdom is different from knowledge, page 49.
Wisdom is to become consciously aware of your subconscious mind, page 50.
Water baptism, page 77.
The Great **White Throne of Judgment**, page 99.

BIBLIOGRAPHY

The following Bible verses displayed in this book were taken from www.biblegateway.com:

Proverbs 3:5-6 NIV, Revelation 17:14 NIV, Revelation 19:16 NIV, Genesis 1:26 NIV, Genesis 1:27 NIV, Genesis 2:1-3 NIV, Genesis 2:5-7 NIV, Genesis 2:16-17 NIV, Genesis 2:18, Genesis 2:19-20 NIV, Genesis 2:21-22 NIV, Genesis 3:2-23, Isaiah 59:2 NIV, Matthew 12:40 NIV, Acts 17:26 NIV, John 16:7, John 16:8-15 NIV, Romans 8:16 NIV, John 8:31-32, Matthew 10:33, Romans 10:9 NIV, Psalm 51 NIV, Matthew 7:15-20 NKJV, Galatians 5:22-24 ESV, Psalm 37:37 NKJV, Matthew 10:34 NKJV, John 10:10 NIV, John 16:33 KJV, Philippians 4:6-7 NKJV, Matthew 11:28-30 NKJV, Proverbs 4:20-22 NIV, Deuteronomy 28:12 NIV, Colossians 1:16 KJV, Deuteronomy 10:14 NIV, John 14:2 KJV, Proverbs 3:6 KJV, 2 Timothy 3:16 KJV, Proverbs 1:7 NIV, 2 Thessalonians 3:3 NIV, Nahum 1:7 NIV, Isaiah 54:17 NKJV, Ephesians 6:10-18 NIV, John 8:44 NIV, 1 Corinthians 2:14-16 ESV, Hebrews 4:12 NIV, Mark 7:21-23 NIV, 1 Samuel 16:7 NIV, 1 Samuel 16:12 NIV, Psalm 139:14 NIV, Genesis 1:31 NIV, Ezekiel 16:10-15 NIV, 1 Peter 5:5-6 NKJV, James 4:10 NKJV, Romans 12:16 NIV, Romans 14:11KJV, John 3:16 NIV, Romans 10:9 NIV, Romans 5:8 NIV, Ezekiel 28:13 KJV, Isaiah 14:12-15 NIV, Revelation 12:4 NIV, Genesis 3:14-15 NIV, John 3:36 NIV, Hosea 4:6 NIV, Psalm 1:1-3 NKJV, 1 Corinthians 6:19 NIV, Galatians 3:26 NIV, 1 Corinthians 3:23 NLT, Hebrew 10:10 NIV, John 10:28-30 NIV, John 10:27 KJV, Romans 8:11 NIV, Matthew 6:25-34 NIV, Proverbs 8:17,18, 21 NIV, Isaiah 53:5 NKJV, Isaiah 53:5 NKJV, Genesis 17:4 NIV, Jeremiah 33:3 NIV, Hebrews 13:8 NIV, John 16:14 NIV, Genesis 1:26 NIV, Genesis 1:28-29 NIV, Psalm 8:4-5 NIV, Psalm 139:13 ESV, Luke

2:22 NIV, Luke 15:10 NIV, Colossians 2:12-14 NIV, Galatians 3:28 NIV, Acts 10:34-35 NIV, 1 Corinthians 13:9-10 NIV, 1 Peter 2:9-10 NIV, 2 Timothy 4:8 NIV, Isaiah 62:3 NIV, 1 Peter 5:4 NIV, Mark 13:32-33 NIV, Corinthians 6:19-20 NIV, Exodus 26 NIV, 1 Chronicles 28:11-12 NIV, 1 King 6 NIV, Revelation 16: 15 NIV, Ephesians 4:26 NIV, 1 Thessalonians 5:2-5 NKJV, Matthew 24:36 ESV, Revelation 19:7-8 NKJV, Revelations 19:11-16 NIV, Colossians 3:23-24 NKJV, 1 Corinthians 13:4-7 NIV, John 4:7-21NIV, 1 Corinthians 7:8-9 NIV, Romans 12:10 ESV, Matthew 5:44 ESV, Matthew 22:35,37,38 NIV, 1 John 5:1-3 NIV, 2 Timothy 3:16-17, Revelation 21:1-5 NKJV, Revelation 21:22-27 NKJV.

Christianity, 'How did Lucifer fall and become Satan?", Web, www.christianity.com, 18th November 2018.

Every Student, *'History of the Bible - Who wrote the Bible?'*, Web, www.everystudent.com, 16th November 2018.

Got questions, *'How long did it take to write the Bible?'*, Web, www.gotquestions.org, 16th November 2018.

Got questions, *'What is wisdom? What is the difference between wisdom and knowledge?',* Web, www.gotquestions.org, 16th November 2018.

Hand, Julie, Bulletproof Blog 16 May 2018, *'Deep Breathing Strengthens Your Brain and Boosts Attention Span, Says New Study'*, Web, https://blog.bulletproof.com, 24th November 2018.

Live Bold & Bloom, *'Breathe Deeply. Live Longer'*. Web, www.liveboldandbloom.com, 24th November 2018.

'Love vs Lust', Web, http://lovevslust.weebly.com, 25th November 2018.

Myers, Catherine, *'Glossary Free Radical'*, Web, www.memorylossonline.com, 15th November 2018.

Pubmed.gov, *'Essential fatty acids and human brain'*, Web, www.ncbi.nlm.nih.gov, 15th November 2018.

Shpungin, Elaine Ph.D., Psychology Today, *'What Happens if You Don't Watch What You Watch?'*, Web, www.psychologytoday.com, 15th November 2018.

Szalay, Jessie, Live Science, 'What Are Free Radicals?', Web, www.livescience.com, 15th November 2018.

Zavada, Jack, ThoughtCo., *'4 Types of Love in the Bible'*, Web, www.thoughtco.com, 25th November 2018.

Morris, Henry, PH.D, 'Garments of Salvation', Web, www.icr.org, 28 June 2019.

www.ingramcontent.com/pod-product-compliance
Lightning Source LLC
Chambersburg PA
CBHW072050290426
44110CB00014B/1619